Community Participation in Tourism Development

Explained Through a Case Study

Who should read the book:

- Students and scholars in the tourism and allied industries
- Practitioners in the industry
- Tourism planning authorities

Dr. Millo Yaja

Dedication

I dedicate this book to my beloved late father, **Shri Millo Lampung**, who was a true social servant and the respected Head Gaon Bura of Tajang Village, Lower Subansiri District, Arunachal Pradesh, India, until his final days.

My father was my pillar of support; he always encouraged my aspirations and offered his support in every way he could. He had accompanied me on a pilot study for my PhD in 2019, a journey that I still cherish today. On April 21, 2023, he peacefully took his last breath, leaving behind a legacy of love, strength, and selfless service.

Contents

List of figures:

List of tables:

Preface

This book draws inspiration and curation from the unique challenges and opportunities of tourism development and community participation in the state of Arunachal Pradesh. The primary goal of the book is to simplify the reading process and facilitate a quick understanding of the local community and tourism development context.

The book uses an in-depth case study to explain its contents and extracts some data from my PhD thesis, which I submitted to Pondicherry University. This makes the book special as it uses authentic data to explain all its content with the very firsthand experiences from the ground. These include various approaches to participation, socio-cultural dimensions, practical understanding, and the support system necessary for tourism development.

Millo Yaja

November 2024

<h2 style="text-align:center">UNIQUE FEATURES OF THE BOOK:</h2>

- **A practical explanation from a case study:** The book explains its contents through research findings. It connects and explains the factors that matter in contemporary business operations.

- **Integrated approach to unique challenges associated with local community and tourism development:** A clear breakdown of barriers to tourism development, such as infrastructural, operational, personal, and socio-cultural barriers. Inclusion of unique challenges faced by local communities in tourism development.

- **Blend of practical and research-based explanation with step-wise process:** Outlines learning outcomes and significance in each chapter. Describes the data collection methods and research process.

- **A comprehensive explanation of the tourism support system:** Examines the support system for local communities in the process of tourism development. Highlights characteristic features of local community-produced tourism products and services.

- **Inclusive insights and interpretations from interviews with the local community:** Presents respondents' views on participating in the tourism industry. Also includes the support systems necessary for tourism development in the destinations.

1. Local Community Participation
and Tourism Development

CHAPTER 1

LOCAL COMMUNITY PARTICIPATION AND TOURISM DEVELOPMENT

<u>Learning Outcomes</u>

The first chapter provides the importance of community participation in tourism development, a brief introduction to Arunachal Pradesh, why the state is relevant as a case, and research problems in the context of tourism in the state. The latter section of the chapter focuses on the selection of respondents and provides a detailed explanation of the criteria and reasoning for selecting individuals or groups to partake in the study. After reading the chapter, you will be able to understand:

- the importance of local community participation in the development of tourism
- the tourism industry in Arunachal Pradesh, including its geography, culture, and significance in the context of tourism
- the specific challenges faced by the tourism sector in Arunachal Pradesh.

1.1 Introduction

Tourism is commonly acknowledged as a significant economic engine on a global scale. Most developed and developing nations equally benefit greatly from the tourism industry. In India, the tourism industry has made significant strides in recent years, which have had an enormous effect on tourist destinations and the nation's overall growth in the economy. While tourism is outgrowing other industries in some tourist hotspots, this development is not the same for all destinations. This phenomenon is due to several reasons. One of the fundamental reasons is the low participation of the local community in tourism development. To ensure integrated tourism development and a greater positive effect, locals must be included in the process of development.

Tosun (2000) argued that community participation is a process that demands adjustment and conformity with open-minded viewpoints that allow the local community to take part in various tourism activities. For inclusive growth and efficient use of local resources throughout the development of tourism, it is essential to involve the community. To begin, let us look at what community participation in tourism means.

__Community participation__ in tourism refers to the involvement of local community members in the tourism development process. Participation encourages locals to share their culture, fairs and festivals, traditional knowledge, customs, etc. with tourists, fostering mutual understanding and respect while earning a livelihood. It's a collaborative approach between residents, tourism governing bodies, and stakeholders to promote cultural heritage, preserve natural environments, and create economic opportunities. Effective community participation in tourism development can lead to more sustainable and responsible tourism practices, benefiting both the local community and the tourism industry as a whole.

The rural economy gets a boost from involving the local community and thereby using resources in tourism planning (Gu & Ryan, 2008). Integration raises the socioeconomic development of the local economy through multiplier effects. The local community may participate in a variety of ways, based on the available local resources and social systems prevailing at a destination. The sustainability of the tourism industry at a destination depends on the social structure and resources available, and sustainability can be achieved through an entrepreneurial approach.

1.2 Local community participation and tourism development

The tourism industry is known to generate employment in dynamic skill sets ranging from unskilled, semi-skilled, skilled, and highly skilled. Each set of employees has opportunities to hold and tasks to do. Those with a combination of all of these abilities have a better chance of finding work in the tourism business. Furthermore, the industry's specific traits accommodate and provide space for a wide range of vocations, allowing many locals to participate. The participation of local people in tourism planning is important since it can be used to gauge the type and extent of participation in the sector. It enhances benefits such as the integration of sociocultural elements into tourism services, representation of the destination, and infrastructure development.

Local community participation in tourism development is a necessary step for inclusive regional development, particularly in developing countries, and it is a necessary component of sustainable tourism (Moscardo et al., 2013; Sutawa, 2012). Most of the time, community tourism businesses struggle to adapt to changing tourism demands and skills (Nair and Hamzah, 2015). Malek and Costa (2015) argued that including the local community in the development and planning of a destination ensures its long-term viability.

1.3 Common challenges for local community participation in tourism development

The inclusion of local people in tourism development decision-making plays an important role in the growth of the tourism industry, creating livelihood opportunities for the locals and generating revenue for destinations. However, there are some challenges related to infrastructural and professional skills for the local community's participation in the tourism industry. Some common dimensions of challenges for local community participation in the tourism industry were extracted from previous studies; all these studies inspired, built the foundation, and shaped the formulation of the current research. These include:

1.3.1   Barriers to tourism development

Barriers to community-based tourism include those related to the development of tourism products and services, marketing, access to capital, and capacity building (Forstner, 2004; Aref, F., 2011; Kala & Bagri,2018). The barriers to tourism are interconnected and strongly correlated with the growth of the industry as a whole (Cole, 2006; Tosun, 2000).

1.3.2   Lack of a common vision for development

A study carried out in Costa Rica by Tasci et al. (2014) revealed that stakeholders lacked a common vision for enhancing community-based tourism. As a result, engaging in the tourism industry can be difficult, particularly for the local population, which has little awareness of the sector, and for destinations that lack the amenities required for tourism development.

1.3.3   Challenges in marketing

Marketing tasks are difficult for local community service providers, and the majority of these service providers rely on third-party stakeholders to sell and promote their tourism products and services.

In other words, local tourism services are incorporated into the greater market pool and offered to customers by third-party organizations such as NGOs, commercial tour operators, guides, and government agencies. Social media in marketing serves as a strategic platform for both the host community and a platform for communication with guests (Chang et al., 2018; Dey & Sarma, 2010; Kachniewska, 2015; Mangold & Faulds, 2009; Wang et al., 2002).

1.3.4 Lack of capacity building and awareness

Briedenhann and Wickens (2004) assert that capacity building should be prioritized, particularly for new tourism businesses, to ensure long-term sustainable development. Capacity building is a requirement for any tourism initiative in remote areas where there is little prior knowledge of tourism and allied businesses boost the business operation. Capacity building serves as a tool for the long-term benefits of sustainable tourist development.

1.3.5   Lack of support and engagement

Authorities' failure to help the local community develop its capabilities is what prevents support and engagement in tourism development (Tasci et al., 2014). As a result, capacity building fosters a favourable attitude toward tourism and gets the locals ready for tourism services. Government agencies can identify gaps in a community's capacity to design a capacity-building program for them to become tourism entrepreneurs. Thereby creating training programs that suit the community to create tourism products and services (Lucchetti & Font, 2011).

1.3.6 Negative impact of tourism

It is possible that the advantages of tourism could occasionally lead to difficulties at the destination for a number of different reasons. Eshliki and Kaboudi (2012) noticed that the town of Ramsar in Iran endured all of the impacts of natural resource distortion left after the tourists departed the destination. Disturbance due to overtourism, ecological impact, cultural differences, etc., between the host community and tourists may result in distinct disputes.

1.3.7 Assistance for business

Due to the constant demands and needs of clients, keeping business running can be difficult at times. The study by Nair and Hamzah (2015) focused on the requirement for efficient procedures to prepare local communities for productive participation in the development of tourism. Seeland (2008) asserts that community-managed micro-enterprises would need the support of local government and may also need assistance through governmental initiatives to keep the local community businesses sustainable. According to a study by Mak et al. (2017), communities welcome outside assistance since it helps them develop the necessary skills to meet market demand for tourism services.

1.3.8 Neglecting opinions of the local community

Numerous organizations involved in the travel and hospitality sectors neglect to take the community's opinions into account and include them in tourism planning (Prabhakaran et al., 2014). In order to build human resources for tourism services at destinations, community involvement must be strong (Gurung & Seeland, 2008; Mize et al., 2016). However, if there is a lack of support and integration of opinion, the local community may become resentful and may not support tourism development. Such a phenomenon might even put the development of the tourism industry in danger (Prabhakaran et al., 2014).

1.3.9   Local community and integration

Tourism in Arunachal Pradesh can significantly change for the better, especially for society. The studies conducted by Patowary and Borgohain (2008) and (Mize et al., 2016) observed that many residents of Ziro Valley in Arunachal Pradesh feel that their views are not incorporated into tourism activities. These studies also point out the importance of integrating local tourism firms and developing awareness about tourism development; otherwise, the opportunities and benefits have been confined to a few segments of society.

1.4 Introduction to Arunachal Pradesh

Arunachal Pradesh is one of India's largest northeastern states, covering an area of 83,743 square kilometres and divided into 25 districts, 26 towns, and 3863 villages (Indian Census, 2011). According to the 2011 Census of India, the state has a population of 13.84 lakh people with a population density of 17 people per square kilometre. Itanagar is the capital city of the state, and it houses various government agencies. It is a populous city because people come from all over the state and neighbouring Indian states for a variety of business and official purposes. Arunachal Pradesh is popularly known as the "Land of Dawn Light Mountains". The state is also known by many names, such as *"Orchid State of India"*, *"Paradise of the Botanists"*, and *"Land of Rising Sun in India"*. **Figure 1.1** shows the political map of Arunachal Pradesh. It is located on the tip of north-east India, surrounded by international borders touching the border with Bhutan (160 km) on the west, China-Tibet on the north and north-east (1,080 km), Myanmar on the eastern side (440 km), and borders with the Indian states of Assam and Nagaland to the south.

Arunachal Pradesh is a land of lush, evergreen forests, deep rivers, hills, sloppy valleys, and beautiful plateaus. The state's area is mainly covered by the Himalayan ranges, with mountains from the northern borders and crisscrossing mountain ranges running north south. These carve up the entire state into five river valleys: *the Kameng, the Lohit, the Subansiri, the Siang, and the Tirap*. The snow from the Himalayan Mountains, countless rivers, and rivulets fed these rivers, except the Tirap, which is mostly fed by the Patkai Range. Saing (Tsangpo in Tibet) is conjoined by the Dibang and the Lohit from the lower areas of Arunachal Pradesh, which transform into the mighty Brahmaputra in Assam that flows into Bangladesh.

Figure 1.1 Map of Arunachal Pradesh

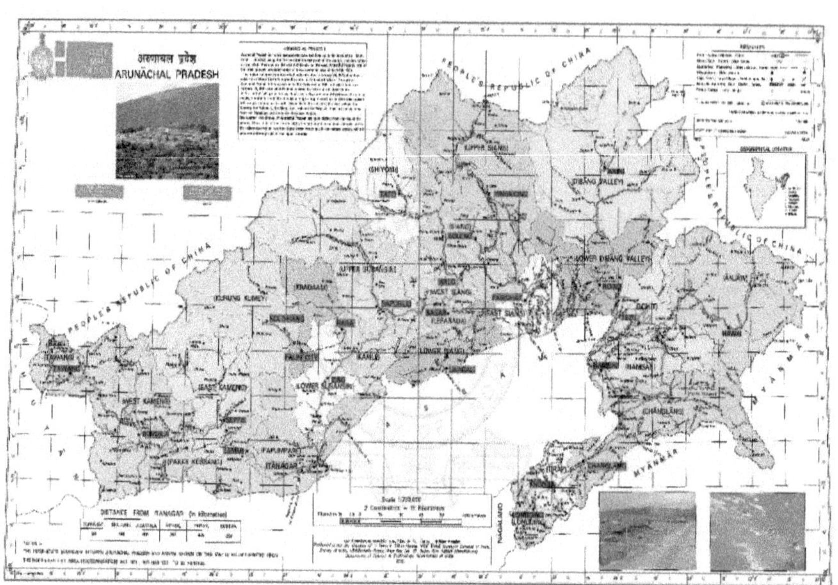

Source: Survey of India
(2023) https://surveyofindia.gov.in/documents/uploads/document-50780-arunachal-state-map.jpg.

The climate of Arunachal Pradesh changes with elevation. One can find windy, cool, and hot to humid climates in low-altitude (100–1500 m) areas; alpine climates are cold and extremely cold in high-altitude areas (3500–5500 m). And one can find extreme colder temperatures in the higher elevations above 5500 m.

1.5 Tourism in Arunachal Pradesh

Arunachal Pradesh is blessed with a unique blend of both natural and cultural diversity. The state has a diverse culture, with 26 major tribes and more than 100 sub-tribes spread across the hillocks and mountains of the state. The geographical isolation allowed these tribes to bloom and evolve differently in terms of customs, traditions, dialects, practices, and expressions in songs, dances, and crafts with distinct identities.

The state offers a complete package that fulfils the thirst of a diverse range of travellers. The area stretches from breath-taking snow-capped mountains in the north to the lush green plains of Brahmaputra Valley in the south. Arunachal is a paradise for botanists due to its wide variety of climbers, shrubs, and pine trees in the tropical rainforest. It is the second largest state covered with forest in the country, next only to Madhya Pradesh, as per the Forest Survey of India (FSI), 2019.

Tourism development in Arunachal Pradesh is in the initial phase, and its development is low-key with respect to tourist arrivals compared to other Indian states and union territories. **Figure 1.2** shows the domestic and foreign tourist arrival data for the 15 years. From the data, it is evident that domestic tourists outnumbered foreign tourists.

Though the tourism industry in Arunachal Pradesh is still in its infancy, it is encouraging to note that, thanks to steps taken by the government and other development agencies in the region, and with this, the local people have begun exploring various business opportunities related to tourism.

Figure 1.2 Tourist Arrival Data of Arunachal Pradesh 2007-2021

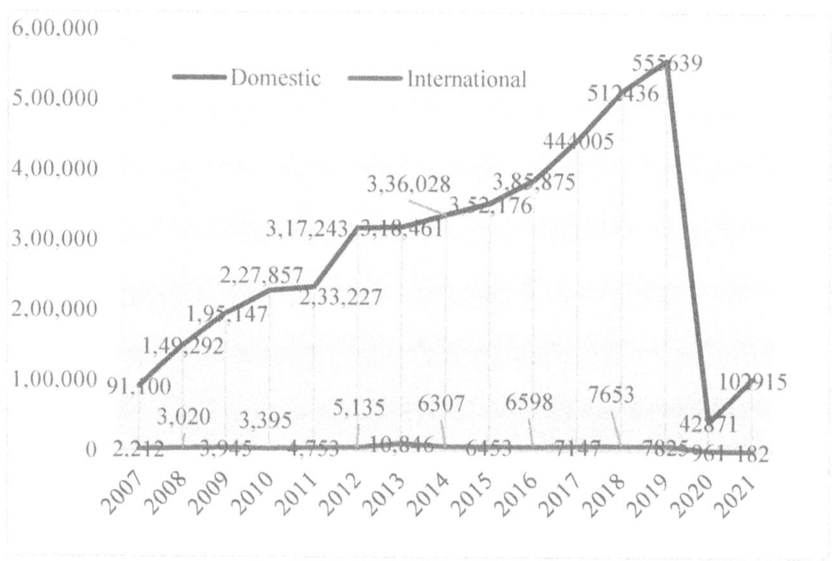

Source: i. Department of Tourism, Government of Arunachal Pradesh (2019): 2007-2019

ii. India Tourism Statistics (2022): 2020-2021

We can see from the data that there is a simultaneous rise in domestic tourist arrivals from 2007 to 2019, though there is a slight fluctuation in the case of foreign tourists. It is important to note that there is a sudden drop in the values of both domestic and foreign tourists for 2020 and 2021, which is due to COVID-19 and other restrictions that affect the global tourism industry.

Arunachal Pradesh has the potential to attract tourists throughout the year owing to its scenic beauty, endowed with a wide range of flora and fauna. The distinctive socio-cultural structure, strategic location, and rich flora and fauna make the state one of the world's important biodiversity hotspots. The vast diversity of resources makes the state an attractive destination for many natural scientists to study and explore.

Due to profound diversity both in natural and cultural resources, Arunachal Pradesh has the potential to be a promising destination for diverse tourists. The stakeholders have recognized the advantages of tourism development in the region due to its cultural and natural resources for tourism development. A few local communities are now recognizing that tourism development is crucial for the state's overall economic development, which is a positive shift in their mindset.

The Directorate of Tourism, Government of Arunachal Pradesh, had already identified 13 tourist circuits over the state's 83,743 square kilometres; these circuits are recognized by the Ministry of Home Affairs, Government of India. Each tourist circuit is distinctive in character, with diverse ethnic cultures, topographies, and vegetation. The tourist destinations in these circuits can be visited throughout the year, as the state of Arunachal Pradesh is blessed with diverse weather types, from windy, hot summers to snowy, chilly winters. Some of the travel seasons are March to June (summer season), with temperatures ranging from 10 to 31°C, July to September (monsoon season) ranging from 19 to 34 °C, and October to February (winter season), where one can expect temperatures ranging from 4°C to -11°C.

The 13 tourist circuits cover important places of interest across the state. The list of these circuits is given below (as of 21st July 2023).

The 13 tourist circuits:

i. Tezpur – Bhalukpong – Bomdila – Tawang

ii. Itanagar – Ziro – Daporijo – Aalo – Pasighat

iii. Pasighat – Jengging – Yingkiong – Tuting

iv. Tinsukia – Tezu – Hayuliang

v. Margherita – Miao – Namdhapa – Vijoynagar

vi. Dibrugarh – Deomali – Hakanjuri – Khonsa

vii. Dibrugarh – Kanubari – Longding

viii. Tezpur – Seijosa – Bhalukpong

ix. Ziro – Palin – Nyapin – Sangram – Koloriang

x. Doimukh – Sagalee – Pake Kessang – Seppa

xi. Aalo – Mechuka

xii. Daporijo – Taliha – Siyum – Nacho

xiii. Jairampur – Manmao – Nampong – Pangsau Pass

Source: Arunachal Tourism, Official Website.

Assessed on 21st July 2023; Link:

https://arunachaltourism.com/

The state is home to the largest monastery in India, Tawang Monastery, and it is also the second largest in the world. The Tawang Monastery is among the few monasteries that were saved from Mao's Cultural Revolution and escaped alteration. The monastery is also known as Ganden Namgyal Lhatse. Along with this, there are two important cultural and historical sites in Arunachal Pradesh on UNESCO's tentative list and are now competing for the status of world heritage sites (accessed on January 16, 2021). One of the two sites is the *Apatani cultural landscape* in Ziro Valley, Lower Subansiri district, and the other is *Thembang Dzong*, a fortified village in West Kameng district.

The tourism industry in India has reached several milestones in the last few years, with a satisfactory increase in tourist arrivals at several Indian tourist destinations. However, the tourism development of Arunachal Pradesh is rather slow. And its growth rate is very negligible as compared to other states in the country. In its quest for development, the state government has recently initiated several measures to uplift tourism by involving local people in various tourism activities in the early 21st century. Accordingly, the region's support system needs to gear up to improve infrastructure and amenities for the smooth operation of tourism services. As such, residents interested in the tourism business must be prepared to integrate with the industry.

1.6 Research problem

Several factors influence the tourist' inflow into Arunachal Pradesh, largely due to its abundant natural and cultural diversity in spite of several inadequacies. There is an urgent need to identify the bottlenecks and enthuse the stakeholders to work on strategies to promote tourism in the region. Keeping in view the diversified nature and multiplicity of tourism services and the benefits that accrue to the local community, it is important to prepare the local community to participate more enthusiastically in scaling up tourism activity in Arunachal Pradesh.

The need to involve the community and encourage participation in tourism has recently been recognized by the state, as has the need for the development of tourism infrastructure and services. As the growth of tourism in the state is at a nascent stage in the region, it is imperative to assess community participation in the tourism development process. Then only tourism in a sustainable and all-inclusive mode is possible.

Another dimension of the study is to examine the challenges in the marketing of community-owned tourism products and services. The impact of modern marketing approaches in this context is a welcome change. The change is quite visible and needs further impetus. In this regard, community participation in tourism in a big way needs no emphasis.

The situation warrants far more attention to the development of tourism from all segments—government, industry captains, and academics. A cursory look at this region enables one to appreciate the various resources waiting to be tapped. If the region's resources are properly converted into tourism products and communicated to the tourism market, it will eventually lead to the creation of value for the rural resources and their optimum utilization.

1.7 Challenges of Arunachal Pradesh Tourism

Arunachal Pradesh, in general, and the study area in particular, lack basic infrastructure worth mentioning for tourism development. It is ironic that, though the state is endowed with picturesque locations that are so unique and offer tremendous scope for tourists to revel, the region has to wait this long to get noticed. The region offers a basket of nature-based tourism products such as ecotourism, wildlife tourism, and educational tourism for botanists and nature lovers. In fact, the whole region is a nature lover's delight. Many natural scientists visit the place for study and exploration. Thanks to their interest and studies, many species of flora and fauna have been discovered in the region in the last few decades.

The unique socio-cultural structure, strategic location, and rich flora and fauna make the state one of the world's top bio-diverse hot spots. The rich resources make the state one of the attractions for many natural scientists to visit in pursuit of their research. This profound diversity in natural and cultural resources makes the state an ideal destination for distinctive interest groups. The state government took cognizance of the interest evinced by nature lovers and got its act together in a focused manner.

There is a general perception in the public that the governments, both at the central and state levels, have not paid much attention to the development of the region, let alone tourism promotion. As a result, the region remained secluded from the outside world for a long time. In the present time, the transportation facilities connecting various parts of the state with the outside world are poor and far from satisfactory. A blessing in disguise, however, is that the state is now connected to Delhi and other parts of the country by train services since 2015. The state needs more air transportation throughout several districts. Nevertheless, in 2022, the capital city, Itanagar, acquired air connections through the establishment of Donyi Polo Airport, also referred to as Hollongi Airport. This development is anticipated to bring significant benefits to the state. A few chopper services are available with limited operations due to its rough terrain. Therefore, the primary transportation network is still primarily through surface transport services. And for many remote villagers, good road connectivity is still a distant dream.

The long-term negligence of the government is one of the reasons often cited by the local public for the inadequate infrastructure in the state. However, with the *'Look East Policy'* (1992), a central government initiative, the state is now poised for improvement in its infrastructure facilities. On the other hand, progress has been slow due to region-specific political issues and turmoil. Many organizations in the state, both government and non-government, are putting in their best efforts to motivate and involve local people in the growth of the state more than ever before.

To visit Arunachal Pradesh, it is mandatory that all domestic and international tourists get an entry permit called an *Inner Line Permit* (ILP) under the Bengal Eastern Frontier

Regulation Act (BEFR), 1873, and the *Protected Area Permits* (PAP) Order, 1958, respectively. However, the state government has eased this process by providing e-ILP for domestic tourists, and ILP can also be obtained on arrival from concerned authorities, while foreign tourists who wish to visit the state are required to obtain a permit from a registered tour operator or directly from government authorities.

1.8 Research gap

Earlier studies, which are few and far between, did not cover tourism-related barriers and their impact on perceptions of tourism development. A broader study on community participation is missing, preventing overall development and leaving less ground for discussion and reaping benefits for the residents from the tourism industry in the state. This is the first study in the state of Arunachal Pradesh as a case study for community participation in tourism.

Considering the need for integration of the local community, which has not yet been addressed in the region, it is felt necessary to understand how local tourism entrepreneurs perceive their involvement in tourism development. There are many reasons and arguments favouring community participation in tourism development. The marketing of a community's tourism products and services needs scholarly attention. Few studies have been done on general tourism marketing services in this domain. However, the marketing of the community's products and services was not touched on in the earlier studies. That aside, it is also necessary to assess any general barriers whatsoever to tourism from the participating local communities and to chalk out appropriate policies to overcome impediments to tourism development.

Given Arunachal's current socio-economic status in terms of the high poverty index of 34.67 per cent, which is much higher than the national average of 21.92 per cent (India Census report, 2011), it is no surprise that the state lagged far behind in infrastructure and consequently industrial development. Therefore, there are hopes that the tourism industry can uplift socio-economic conditions to a greater extent with proper integration of the local community in the development process.

Since tourism is a multi-dimensional and multi-faceted industry, tourism promotion in any destination leads to creating economic opportunities in various spheres like transport, the accommodation sector, and various allied commercial establishments that cater to tourists' needs. The tourism industry is a highly people-intensive industry, and therefore the need for capacity-building programs in various tourism-related activities is more pronounced now than ever before.

Since tourism is a multi-dimensional and multi-faceted industry, tourism promotion in any destination leads to creating economic opportunities in various spheres like transport, the accommodation sector, and various allied commercial establishments that cater to tourists' needs. Needless to say, the tourism industry is a highly people-intensive industry, and therefore the need for capacity-building programs in various tourism-related activities is more pronounced now than ever before.

1.9 Summary

The chapter explored the unique characteristics of Arunachal Pradesh, including its geographical traits and diverse cultural heritage, why it is relevant, and why it has been used as a case study to explain many common challenges for community participation in tourism development. The contents of the chapter provided readers with an understanding of the distinctive combination of elements that enhance opportunity and challenges in the broader area of local community and tourism development that are occurring in many countries.

Furthermore, the chapter highlighted the insight into the difficulties faced by the tourism sector, presenting a thorough comprehension of the problems that must be resolved to ensure the industry's continuous expansion. In the next chapter, we will understand the objectives considered for the study, the significance of community participation, the research approach, and the methodology used.

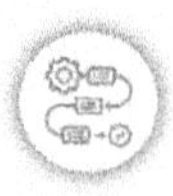

2. Research Approach and Methodology

CHAPTER 2
RESEARCH APPROACH AND METHODOLOGY

Learning Outcomes

This chapter provides the objectives of the research overview, why the research is conducted, the research approach, and the methodology used to address specific issues in the context of community participation in tourism. A research objective is a clear and concise statement that defines a primary research goal. It outlines what the researcher hopes to achieve or investigate, serving as a guiding principle for the entire research process, and after reading the chapter, you will be able to understand:

- need of the study, objectives, and significance
- the process of selecting appropriate data sources, and samples
- the process of selecting respondents or participants for research and the considerations involved, such as representativeness from different types of tourism firms
- the role of a pilot study in refining research methodologies and tools, helping to improve the overall quality of the study, including both quantitative and qualitative approaches.

2.1 Introduction

Earlier studies have associated community participation in tourism with areas like sustainable tourism, ecotourism, social capital, socio-economic development, preservation of the natural and cultural heritage of the destination, and so on. However, various dimensions of the local community's participation in tourism entrepreneurship and integration of locals during tourism promotion and development of products and services are still a new area. For example, the nature of participation and the integration of locals in initiatives of both public and private tourism agencies; another one is the visibility issues of local tourism products and services, which have largely remained unexplored and need scholarly intervention.

2.2 The need for study

Previous research on community participation has primarily focused on policymakers' perspectives and the relevance of participation in tourism while little attention is paid to the local community's thoughts and perceptions of tourism development. Previous research had barely touched on the marketing of locally produced and owned tourism products and services. As a result, it is necessary to investigate how tourism products and services are planned, produced, and disseminated by the local community service providers. Most big players in the tourism business fail to consider and incorporate the community's views in tourism planning (Prabhakaran et al., 2014). This breeds negative sentiments and emotions that impact overall tourism development.

According to Brouder and Eriksson (2013), a lack of understanding in the tourism industry serves as a barrier for locals to enter the high-end business. According to Goodwin (2002), a lack of capital, as well as proper awareness, deters the local community, and as a result, they play second fiddle in the entire spectrum of tourism development. Reed (1997) emphasized the significance of power in building the correct ecosystem as well as the function of government as a facilitator. Therefore, some of the key areas have been selected that need special emphasis and are relevant to the current phase of tourism development in the state of Arunachal Pradesh. The areas considered for research are also relevant to new tourism destinations and emerging destinations in developing countries. These are:

2.2.1 Barriers to tourism development from local community perspectives

Barriers to tourism are often related to the sustainability of tourism businesses and development. The sustainability of tourism in the region broadly needs a genuine opportunity given to the host community by allowing them to participate through a bottom-up development model

(Coros et al., 2017; Hall, 1998). Further, fostering entrepreneurial spirit in the local community is the need of the hour (Triantafillidou &Tsiaras, 2018). The nature of barriers to tourism varies depending on the level of the product's life cycle and the host's socio-cultural structure. Quite often, barriers may be region-specific too. In this regard, the different types of barriers we are going to discuss in the other subsequent chapters of the book.

2.2.2 Building capacity and its requirement

Building capacity is required for active community participation. Many local tourism authorities and agencies, however, ignore tourism planning in a professional manner and are ineffective in instituting the appropriate capacity-building programs, even though the local community requires knowledge, expertise, and skills to establish and organize business entities (Bello et al., 2018). Acharya and Halpenny (2013) conducted a study in rural Nepal and discovered that capacity building stimulates the establishment of diverse traditional businesses for long-term community development. Capacity building in operational areas of business, as well as training in creating and marketing artefacts, cooking, and baking skills, assists locals in establishing tourism-related companies.

According to Carlisle et al. (2013), capacity-building fosters the proper attitude toward entrepreneurship and innovation by bringing a positive perspective from tourism service providers in tourism and allied firms, which may eventually lead to a contribution to the growth of tourism. However, there is still much to be discovered regarding the function of capacity building and instilling professionalism in the local population in order for them to be successful in tourism business ventures.

2.2.3 Integration of local communities in tourism development

Integration of local communities is challenging in developing countries (Chiutsi & Saarinen, 2017), and the barriers to integration change according to the nature of the destination and the level of participation of local communities in tourism. To create an inclusive model of local community participation in tourism, proper integration of the local population is crucial (Gu & Ryan, 2008). Thus, in a way, integration of local culture and tradition is necessary to achieve sustainable development (Shen et al., 2008). Therefore, proper integration entails the inclusion of local culture, traditions, and values in tourism development.

2.2.4 Integration of locals' view in tourism development

Several studies have identified that the integration of local communities into tourism creates new economic opportunities and more activities for tourists at destinations (Saarinen & Lenao, 2014). Tosun and Jenkins (1998) also observed that integrated tourism planning calls for tourism markets to be subnational, national, or international in the establishment of linkages between tourism development agencies and the local community. However, Saxena and Ilbery (2008) commented that many studies reported a lack of coordination in policymaking, which is the principal reason for inadequate attention to the local community and their views on tourism development.

The existing literature is extensive on integrating the local community into tourism planning and development, paving the way for successful partnerships for a better economy. However, service providers' participation in various forums related to tourism and its effect on integration have not been studied systematically and have yet to find a prominent place in the existing literature. Hence, the current study also focuses on this gap.

2.2.5 Challenges in meeting the demands of the industry

Local tourism service providers often face challenges in adapting to the changing demands of their work and the skills required to perform it effectively (Nair & Hamzah,

2015). For example, Luo and Lee (2017) found that Aboriginal people in Taiwan lack decision-making skills and confidence, as exhibited in various meetings related to tourism development for livelihoods. The corporate culture and methods of communication in transforming traditional knowledge of the local community quite often contribute to conflicts and ad hoc decision-making in tourism development (Munar, 2012; Prince, 2017). These studies show that a lack of professional skills may prevent meeting the demands of the industry.

2.2.6 Marketing approach for community tourism products and services

Many developing nations often aim for a strategic marketing approach for destination planning and development and identify an image to represent the place (Chen et al., 2013; Moertini, 2012). Furthermore, images, themes, and words used during tourism promotion for any destination become 'identity' and 'brand' for a long time.

An examination of developing nations' tourism markets and marketing patterns reveals that a distinct and systematic study for each region is essential, as each place and the variables are distinct (Echtner and Prasad, 2003). Another study done by Zeng and Gerritsen (2014) observes that social media in tourism marketing is still in its infant stage, and in the days to come, the role of social media in the tourism industry will be immense. Hence, this is one of the important areas where locally produced tourism products and services should be explored in depth for effective marketing and communication.

2.2.7 Residents' attitude and sustainable tourism development

To achieve sustainable tourism, understanding residents' attitudes toward tourism development in their locality and the well-being of residents is a prerequisite while planning for tourism development (Amir et al., 2015; Hrvatska & Kilipiris, 2005; Saufi et al., 2014). Choi & Murray (2010) argued that the lack of a long-term approach to planning hampers business sustainability.

Through different plans and initiatives, government authorities encourage the local community to participate in tourism and related services. However, local service providers are often unable to compete with other high-end firms, resulting in fewer tourists, lower income, and, in some circumstances, a loss of service identity. As a result, this study looks into how regional tourism businesses create and market their community tourism services and goods. The research also aims to provide a fundamental understanding of the market system and the development of locally produced tourism products and services.

2.3 The major research problem outlined for the study

Previous research on community-based tourism has largely focused on the benefits and importance of local community participation in tourism development, while this study focuses on local community tourism entrepreneurs and tourism-allied businesses that are locally owned and controlled by the local community. The study's purpose is to learn about the barriers and concerns of local tourism firms. Furthermore, Arunachal Pradesh has a large potential for tourism research and development. The nascent stage of tourism development creates more room, especially in locals' perceptions of tourism development, and access challenges local community participation.

The community in the region has recently begun to experience a boom in tourism-related business opportunities in the related industry. Thus, the perspective of tourism from local service providers would have a significant impact on the future development of tourism in Arunachal Pradesh. Since the study is time-bound due to the multiple dimensions and issues related to tourism development and community participation, the following major concerns are churned out for the study:

- Arunachal Pradesh, as a whole, despite its abundant natural and cultural diversity, has yet to make a significant mark on the tourism development map of India.

- Many areas in the region are gearing up for tourism activities where community participation is merely passive, and in some cases, it is absent from the planning process. This led to the exclusion of the local community's views and opinions from tourism activities.

- Despite the poor accessibility and lack of tourism infrastructure in many places in the region, tourism activities are happening at a low level, where a need for skilled human resources at the local level is to be explored in depth to make reasonable improvements.

- There are gaps in channelling the efforts of tourism authorities and community stakeholders, which can prevent the sustainable growth of tourism in the region.

2.4 Objectives of the study

Considering the current stage of tourism development in Arunachal Pradesh, the existing research gaps, and the major concerns, the present study is pursued with the following objectives:

1. To find out the nature and type of local community participation in tourism in the select tourism destinations of Arunachal Pradesh.
2. To understand the extent of integration of local tourism service providers in the development of tourism in the state.
3. To assess and understand the barriers, if any, faced by service providers of the region for effective integration.
4. To explore the marketing opportunities of community-produced/owned tourism products and services; and
5. To seek the views of local service providers about their aspirations and experience in tourism.

2.5 Significance of the Study

The state of Arunachal Pradesh rarely receives scholarly attention from a tourism perspective. The importance of involving community participation in tourism and the integration of the locals in tourism development in Arunachal Pradesh remained, by and large, an untouched area of study. Given the importance of the local community, it is disheartening to note that its participation is low. The reason for less participation may be due to a variety of reasons. Therefore, it is high time that the barriers to participation encountered by the local community are explored.

The primary reason could also be due to a lack of awareness and ignorance about the benefits of tourism. Therefore, the present study focuses on the support system for tourism and the extent of the integration of local communities in the tourism development process. The significance of the study can be illuminated with the following points:

- The study maps how local service providers are integrated with capacity-building programs in tourism destinations.
- attempts to understand how community-produced tourism products and services are marketed;
- helps to understand how tourism services are marketed to tourists;
- explores the support systems and identifies possible barriers to tourism development;
- also identifies other tourism ventures in which the residents could be involved, which facilitates the growth of local enterprises.

2.6 Sample districts

Five districts of the state were considered for data collection based on the participation of the local community in tourism activities by the Department of Tourism, Government of Arunachal Pradesh (www.arunachaltourism.com). The five districts are Lower Subansiri, Papum Pare, Tawang, West Kameng, and West Saing. **Figure 2.1** shows selected districts of the state. Data was collected from homestays, hotels, local performing artists, tour guides, tour operators, souvenir shops, and transport service providers.

Figure 2.1 Five districts' location on the map of Arunachal Pradesh

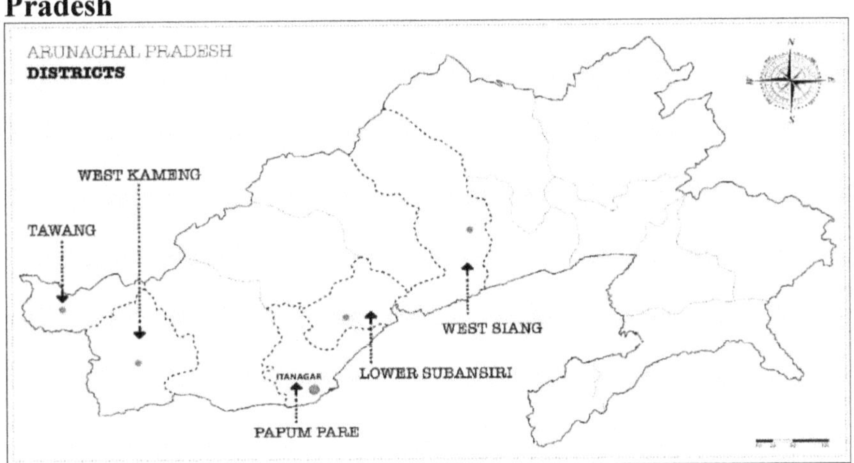

The map is marked with icons for selected districts. This map is only for representative purposes and is not to be scaled. Adapted from source:- Official website of Arunachal Pradesh, https://www.arunachalpradesh.gov.in/ accessed on 15th January 2021.

2.7 Pilot study

The Lower Subansiri district of the state was chosen as the pilot study due to the high concentration of local tourism and allied businesses. The pilot study was conducted in 2018 between September and November to assess the validity of the questionnaire with a sample of 40 locals participating in the tourism industry. Key resource persons like Tourism officials, Local community leaders, the Shelf Help Group associated with tourism, and concerned officials of the Department of Forests and the Department of Textile & Handicrafts were met, and their views and suggestions were obtained and incorporated in the final questionnaire. The variables for the study were selected from a literature review and from multiple field visits prior to the final collection of data.

2.8 Data collection time frame

During the study period, it was found that 135 tourism service units, which include homestays, hotels, and tour operators, were listed on Arunachal Tourism's website in these five selected districts. However, during data collection, non-registered, registration-under-process service providers, local tour guides, performing artists, souvenir shops, and transport service providers not registered or listed with the directorate of tourism in the state were also included in the study to incorporate the maximum number of respondents without compromising the objectives of the study. The researcher met and interviewed resource persons, respondents, and officials concerned with tourism and allied services in Arunachal Pradesh between September 2018 and September 2019 and followed up on the same until July 2021, wherever required.

2.9 Selection of Respondents

The districts for the sample were selected on the basis of the number of Tourism service units hosted on the Arunachal Tourism website as of 31st August 2018. Arunachal Tourism Arunachal Tourism is the official website of the Directorate of Tourism, Government of Arunachal Pradesh, at www.arunachaltourism.com

(31st August 2018). Five districts were selected for data collection based on higher concentrations of tourist units: Lower Subansiri, Papumpare, Tawang, West Kameng, and West Saing.

The respondents of the study are the local community members participating in tourism-related economic activity and allied services with established businesses to make a living. The tourism service units include accommodation (Hotels & Resorts), Homestays, and Tour Operators in the state. However, during the data collection process, other tourism professionals who participate in the tourism businesses, such as local Guides, Souvenir shops, Transport Service providers, and Local performing artists who have not registered themselves with the tourism department but have started the services, were also included in the survey.

The data collection was restricted to only local communities that are directly engaged in tourism-related businesses. However, the local community working as tourism officials in the state tourism department were not considered respondents to the study; however, they were considered key resource persons or informants while gathering official data related to tourism in the state.

2.10 Data collection method and process

The data was collected using a purposive sampling method in the initial phase, and later, it became snowball sampling. Tourism service units, which are listed on the official website of the state department, were taken as leads for identifying other respondents like local Guides, Souvenir shops, Transport Services, and Local performing Artists who are not listed with the tourism department. The reason for including these services is to incorporate their views and reach out to the maximum number of participants.

Snowball's method of data collection was adopted for non-registered service units. 450 local community members participated in the survey who are involved in tourism and allied businesses. However, 421 samples were considered for final analysis. The **survey questionnaire** was used along with semi-structured questions in the interview to support scale-based items. Since the study is a mixed-methods approach, the questionnaire comprises both quantitative and qualitative questions.

2.11 Statistical tools used and stepwise research process

For open-ended questions and semi-structured questions, qualitative data analysis is used. Thematic analysis for comments and interviews was carried out for responses regarding opinions and barriers specific to the service providers for tourism in the region. Statistical tools, including, mean, standard deviation, frequency, and percentage analysis, were used using SPSS 21 software for quantitative data analysis. The research was carried out using a stepwise process as shown in **Figure 2.2**.

Figure 2.2 Stages of Research Process

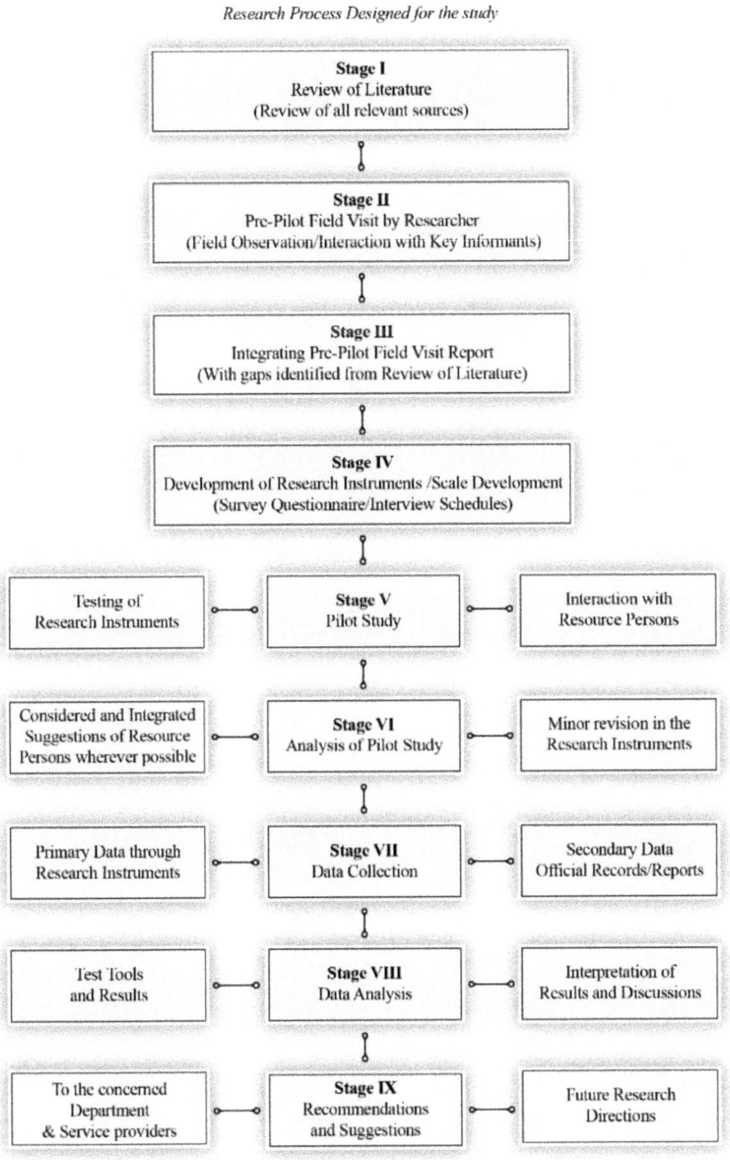

Research Process Designed for the study

Stage I
Review of Literature
(Review of all relevant sources)

Stage II
Pre-Pilot Field Visit by Researcher
(Field Observation/Interaction with Key Informants)

Stage III
Integrating Pre-Pilot Field Visit Report
(With gaps identified from Review of Literature)

Stage IV
Development of Research Instruments /Scale Development
(Survey Questionnaire/Interview Schedules)

Testing of Research Instruments — **Stage V** Pilot Study — Interaction with Resource Persons

Considered and Integrated Suggestions of Resource Persons wherever possible — **Stage VI** Analysis of Pilot Study — Minor revision in the Research Instruments

Primary Data through Research Instruments — **Stage VII** Data Collection — Secondary Data Official Records/Reports

Test Tools and Results — **Stage VIII** Data Analysis — Interpretation of Results and Discussions

To the concerned Department & Service providers — **Stage IX** Recommendations and Suggestions — Future Research Directions

Source: Author's creation

2.12 Summary

This chapter has explored the research design and approaches used in the study. These include introducing study locations, objectives, significance, data sources, methodology used, research instruments, and selection of respondents. It is believed and intended that the research process and approaches used for the study could contribute to achieving the objectives of the study.

By explaining the process of selecting sample districts, the rationale behind their selection, and how they accurately represent the larger study area, the chapter further elaborated on the contextual background for the research. The next chapter discusses respondents' demographic profile and the nature of their participation in tourism development.

3. Demographic and Nature of Participation

CHAPTER 3

DEMOGRAPHIC AND NATURE OF PARTICIPATION

<u>Learning Outcomes</u>

This chapter presents data analysis, such as demographic characteristics of respondents, types of tourism activities, and the nature of community participation. The chapter also outlines community members' specific roles and initiatives in the tourism industry. The chapter also includes interpreting the primary data and an overview of tourism development. After finishing the chapter, you will gain the following understanding:

- different types of participation from locals in tourism-related activities
- demographic features of the respondents
- the nature of local community participation in the tourism sector
- the existing tourism activities in the region.

3.1 Introduction

In this chapter, we'll learn about demographic, the nature of community tourism participation, and tourism activities before moving on to interpretation. These results are quantitative primary data, which will help us navigate and connect other data discussed in the book's subsequent chapters. The study's complete data is categorized into qualitative and quantitative data. Quantitative data is analyzed with the help of Statistical Packages for Social Sciences (SPSS version 21). The survey questionnaires and semi-structured interviews are analyzed per the study's objectives. Thematic analysis for qualitative data, such as semi-structured questions, interviews, and comments, was done accordingly, which we will discuss in later chapters of the book.

3.2 Demographic characteristics of respondents

The demographic composition of a sample population can significantly influence the results. Demographic data provide essential context for interpreting the characteristics of the study sample. For instance, social science research findings based on a predominantly urban, high-income sample might not apply to rural, low-income populations. Incorporating these aspects of diverse demographic representation into research promotes equity and inclusivity by providing a broader understanding of the study sample.

In this research, 450 respondents participated. Of the 450 participants, 421 were found to be complete in all respects, and as such, 421 were considered for final analysis. The demographic profile of the respondents plays an important role in participation in tourism and allied services. Demographic factors include the age, gender, marital status, occupation, monthly income, and educational qualifications of the respondents. It was found that the participation of male respondents was higher than that of female respondents. Table 3.1 indicates that 61.5% of the 421 respondents are men and 38.5% are women. A little more than one-third (37.1%) of the sample respondents were 18 to 28 years old.

From **Table 3.1**, it may be noted that 61% of the sample respondents are married. Almost half of the population (49.6%) is in the below-Rs 10,000 monthly income group. 27% of the respondents are in the income range of 10,001–20,000, 17% in 20,001–40,000, and only 6% are in 40,001 and above.

Table 3.1 Demographic Characteristics of Respondents

N-421 Category	Frequency	Percentage	Category	Frequency	Percentage
Gender			**Monthly Income (Indian Rupees)** Less than 10,000	209	**49.6**
Female	162	38.5	10,001-20,000	115	27.3
Male	259	**61.5**	20,001-40,000	73	17.3
Age (Years)			40,001 and above	24	5.7
18-28	156	**37.1**			
29-38	131	31.1			
39-48	70	16.6	**Education Qualification**		
49 and above	64	15.2	No formal Education	43	10.2
Occupation			Primary	115	27.3
Farmer	115	27.3	Secondary	122	29.0
Govt./PSU	44	10.5	Graduation	116	**27.6**
Private Job	114	27.1	Post-Graduation and above	25	5.9
Self Employed	148	**35.2**			
Marital Status Married	257	**61.0**			
Unmarried	164	39.0			

Source: Yaja, M. (2021) Community participation in tourism a case study of Arunachal Pradesh.

Many participants in the survey are from primary, secondary, and graduate levels of education, constituting 27.3%, 29.0%, and 27.6%, respectively. 10% of the respondents had no formal education; interestingly, only 6% are post-graduates in different disciplines. The tourism industry in the state is currently in its infant stage, and all participants are first-generation entrepreneurs. The participants in the various tourism services are from different occupations. For example, 27% are from farming, while another 27% are from private jobs, 35% of respondents are self-employed, and only 10% are from government and public sector undertakings (PSU).

3.3 Key respondents

Participants in the survey are associated with various tourism service units, broadly classified under seven categories: homestays, hotels, tour operators, tour guides, transport services, souvenir shops, and local performing artists. Homestays and hotels constitute 26% each, and transport services, tour operators, performing artists, tour guides, and souvenir shops constitute 18%, 9%, 7%, 6%, and 8%, respectively, as shown in **Table 3.2.**

Table 3.2 Key Respondents

Units	Frequency	Percent
Homestay	110	26.1
Hotel	110	26.1
Transport Service	75	17.8
Tour Operator	36	8.6
Souvenir Shop	35	8.3

Performing Artist	31	7.4
Tour Guide	24	5.7
Total	**421**	**100.0**

Source: Yaja, M. (2021) Community participation in tourism a case study of Arunachal Pradesh

The key respondents of the study are homestays, Hotels, Transport Services, Tour Operators, Souvenir Shops, Tour Guides, and local Artists who organize and perform special cultural events for tourists. These respondents are local farmers operating some forms of tourism services or others. Some government and PSU employees are also engaged in tourism activities, though the number is relatively low. Respondents also include employees from the private sector and self-employed people. Employees in the Directorate of Tourism, Govt. of Arunachal Pradesh, were not considered respondents. However, the researcher met with them to procure official data and information during the study.

3.4 Nature of participation in tourism services

This research established community participation in tourism services for the first time in Arunachal Pradesh. Most locals, constituting 68.4%, participate in tourism services as a primary occupation, while the remaining 31.6% have a secondary occupation, as shown in Table 3.3. Further, as seen in Table 3.3, three-fourths of the male respondents took tourism as their primary occupation. Interestingly, more than half of the female respondents were found to take up tourism-related activities as a primary occupation to supplement family income.

Table 3.3 Nature of participation in Tourism * Gender Crosstabulation

Nature of participation	Gender				Total	Percent
	Female	Percent	Male	Percent		
Tourism as Primary Occupation	92	56.8	196	75.7	288	68.4
Tourism as Secondary Occupation	70	43.2	63	24.3	133	31.6
Total	**162**	**100.0**	**259**	**100.0**	**421**	**100.0**

Source: Yaja, M. (2021) Community participation in tourism a case study of Arunachal Pradesh

3.5 Gender wise participation in various tourism services

The interpretation of gender-wise participation in various tourism services is critical for several reasons, spanning economic, social, and developmental aspects. **Table 3.4** provides an indication of male and female respondents' participation in the various types of businesses in this study. Approximately two-thirds of female respondents operate homestays and manage souvenir shops, with a few also pursuing performing arts, as they find the home environment more comfortable. On the other hand, the majority of male respondents (73.6%) work in hotels, transport services, and as tour operators and guides.

Table 3.4 Types of Tourism businesses * Gender wise distribution

Types of Tourism businesses	Gender		Total
	Female	**Male**	
Homestay	70	40	110
Hotel	29	81	110
Transport Service	03	72	75
Tour Operator	11	25	36
Souvenir Shop	26	09	35
Performing Artist	21	10	31
Tour Guide	02	22	24
Total	**162**	**259**	**421**

Source: Yaja, M. (2021) Community participation in tourism a case study of Arunachal Pradesh

Interpreting gender-inclusive participation in this study will ensure that tourism services cater to a broader audience, offering products and experiences that appeal to different genders. This inclusivity can attract a wider range of tourists and enhance customer satisfaction. It also helps break down gender stereotypes and norms, fostering a more inclusive society. Gender diversity in tourism services can lead to a more comprehensive understanding of customer needs and preferences, as well as their engagement with different tourism businesses. Women and men may bring different insights into service delivery, improving the quality and variety of tourism experiences that help to create diverse perspectives in businesses.

3.6 Participation of the local community in tourism firms

Table 3.4 denotes the types of tourism firms the locals have taken up in the region. Most locals have taken the profession of tourism as a primary occupation, and accommodation service is the preferred segment of business for many, followed by transport service. However, the comments from the respondents suggest critical issues and gaps in the transportation business in the region, a topic we will delve into further in the later part of this book. The benefits of the transportation business are not adequately channelled to benefit the locals, and quite often outsiders snatch away business from locals in the transport segment.

The results also show a shortage of tourist guides, which is why service providers have made alternatives like hiring school teachers or local youth, and sometimes drivers also act as guides. Despite several training programs conducted for tourist guides by the state tourism department, surprisingly, the official tourism portal of the state government does not contain even a single registered guide. The situation calls for immediate action, so much so that many local youths are picked up and inducted as tour guides, equipping them with the necessary skills.

Prevailing tourism activities are, by and large, confined to rural and cultural tourism in the region. Nature-based activities, such as trekking and farm visits, are low-key. Despite rich potential and adequate local talent, the area lacks other visitor-engaging activities like experiential tourism activities like handloom and craft making. Another critical point to note about tourist activities is that, despite tourism department's aggressive promotion of *adventure tourism*, adventure-centric tourism activities are few and far between (Table 3.5).

3.7 Tourism Activities in the Region

To understand the perceptions of respondents about various tourism activities in the region top tourism activities are ranked in **Table:3.5**. The ranked 1 indicates the top activity or the common tourism activities happening in the region, and on the other hand, the ranked 12 indicates the least preferred activity that is happening in the region.

Table 3.5 Popular existing tourism activities in the region

N-421 Statements	M	SD	N %	R %	S %	O %	A %	Mean Rank
Interacting with local community	4.04	.880	.4	4.0	15.9	**46.1**	32.5	1
Visiting Sacred & Ritual sites	3.99	.983	0	9.0	21.6	30.6	**38.7**	2
Trying local cuisine	3.88	.890	0	8.1	22.1	**43.7**	26.1	3
Trekking & Nature Walk	3.78	.781	.5	5.5	24.5	**54.6**	15.0	4
Visiting farm/agriculture field	3.38	.856	.2	16.2	36.6	**39.2**	7.8	5
Listening to local folklore	3.26	1.017	1.0	27.6	28.0	**31.8**	11.6	6
Visiting zoos/wildlife/sanctuaries	3.14	.980	2.1	26.1	**36.3**	26.1	9.3	7
Visiting crafts centre & museum	3.01	.977	1.2	36.1	**31.1**	24.0	7.6	8
Adventure/Mountaineering/ Rafting	2.56	.686	1.7	**48.7**	42.5	5.9	1.2	9
Visiting on study purposes	2.52	.735	2.4	**52.0**	39.7	2.9	3.1	10
Trying local handloom/crafts items	2.35	.955	15.9	**48.0**	25.4	6.9	3.8	11
Volunteering to teach in schools/communities	1.29	.602	**75.8**	22.1	.7	.5	1.0	12

Source: Yaja, M. (2021) Community participation in tourism a case study of Arunachal Pradesh
Mean=M, Std. Deviation=SD, Never=N, Rarely=R, Sometimes=S, Often=O, Always=A
Mean*: The higher the mean (M) score, the stronger the agreement is with the given statements.

The respondents were asked on a 5-point Likert Scale to give their preferences on statements. For example, Never=N, Rarely=R, Sometimes=S, Often=O, and Always=A for the 12 different tourist activities as shown in Table 3.6. The most preferred option among the tourism activities from the given list is "Interacting with the local community" (M = 4.04). 46.1% of the respondents found it often happens in the region. This is followed by "Visiting Sacred & Ritual Sites" (M = 3.89), as 38.7% of the respondents observed it as always happening in the region.

From the mean rank, it is found that "Volunteering to teach in schools/communities" is the least preferred activity by the tourists in the region. The lower Mean not only symbolizes the least preferred activities but may also be interpreted as an area of opportunity that needs attention from stakeholders.

Types of tourism activities in the study region:

1. Interacting with local community
2. Visiting Sacred & Ritual sites
3. Trying local cuisine
4. Trekking & Nature Walk
5. Visiting farm/agriculture field
6. Listening to local folklore
7. Visiting zoos/wildlife/sanctuaries
8. Visiting crafts centre & museum
9. Adventure/Mountaineering/ Rafting
10. Visiting on study purposes
11. Trying local handloom/crafts items
12. Volunteering to teach in schools/communities

- **Interacting with the local community:**

   Interaction with the local culture and community builds and helps acquire a deeper understanding of the local way of life. It may involve conversations, cultural exchanges, or participation in community activities respecting sacred sites and supporting local businesses and conservation efforts. These activities enhance the travel experience and promote responsible and sustainable tourism.

- **Visiting sacred & ritual sites:**

  Tourists visit sacred and ritualistic sites, such as temples, churches, monasteries, mosques, or other places of religious or cultural significance. It provides insight into the local community's spiritual and cultural practices.

- **Trying local cuisine:**

  One of the joys of travel is sampling the local food. Trying indigenous cuisine is an intriguing and blissful activity during any trip or vacation. Trying local cuisine to experience the flavours and getting hands-on training in a region's culinary traditions can be a memorable part of a trip.

- **Trekking & nature walk:**

  Trekking & nature walk activities entail exploring natural landscapes on foot. Trekking typically refers to lengthier, more difficult hikes, whereas nature walks are shorter, less strenuous excursions through scenic areas. Both provide a more intimate relationship with nature and the environment of destinations.

- **Visiting farm/agriculture fields:**

  Tourists can visit farms or agricultural fields to learn about local farming practices and crop cultivation and partake in activities such as harvesting and planting. This is a hands-on method for understanding the significance of agriculture in the region and ways to create a unique experience for tourists.

- **Listening to local folklore:**

  Immersing oneself in local folklore and storytelling can be a delightful way to learn about a destination's history, mythology, and legends. Frequently, locals have fascinating experiences to share.

- **Visiting zoos/wildlife/sanctuaries:**

  Visiting these places holds special significance for a tourist. It is a way to create learning awareness, provide opportunities to see wildlife for those interested in wildlife, and also promote the conservation of animal species.

- **Visiting crafts centre & museum:**

  Exploring crafts centres and museums allows travellers to appreciate the artistic and cultural heritage of a region. It frequently involves observing and purchasing handcrafted goods and works of art.

- **Adventure/mountaineering/rafting:**

  Thrill-seeking tourists who partake in mountaineering, rafting, or other extreme sports experience a surge of adrenaline. These activities highlight the destination's natural grandeur and adventure opportunities.

- **Visiting for study purposes:**

Travelling to a destination for educational or research purposes enables individuals to delve profoundly into a particular subject, be it history, culture, ecology, or any other field.

- **Trying local handloom/crafts items:**
  Supporting local artisans by purchasing handcrafted items, such as textiles, pottery, jewellery, and souvenirs, is a way to contribute to the local economy and bring home one-of-a-kind recollections.

- **Volunteering to teach in schools/communities:**
  Volunteering to teach in local schools or communities is a meaningful way to give back to the destination. It enables travellers to interact with locals and contribute to community development and education.

3. Summary

In this chapter, we have seen the demographic characteristics of the participants, providing variables such as age, occupation, and nature of participation in tourism businesses. This information provided a comprehensive profile of the respondents included in the study, which we will connect to and discuss further in the following chapters. This entails a thorough investigation of their participation in the tourism sector and lays the groundwork for a comprehensive explanation of the community's influence on tourism development and vice versa. The chapter included a qualitative examination of how community members actively participate in and influence the tourism industry, providing a broader view of their engagement. In the next chapter, we will look into different types of barriers to tourism development and the challenges of local communities while participating in tourism development.

4. Barriers to Tourism Development and Participation

CHAPTER 4
BARRIERS TO TOURISM DEVELOPMENT AND PARTICIPATION

<u>Learning Outcomes</u>

his chapter discusses the barriers to community participation in the tourism industry and other barriers that prevent tourism development. Tourism development is improving and expanding tourism infrastructure and services to attract more tourists. The chapter also includes excerpts from respondents' interviews, clearly articulating and expressing various barriers. These barriers prevent local communities from actively participating in tourism development or fully realizing their potential. Readers can relate to similar difficulties or barriers in other destinations after understanding the various types of barriers to tourism growth and community participation. After reading the chapter, you will be able to understand:

- infrastructural, operational, personal, and socio-economic barriers
- different types of barriers faced by local community tourism service providers in both quantitative and qualitative manners
- intensity of these barriers based on different parameters
- how these barriers prevent active participation
- different perspectives from respondents on barriers to tourism development.

4.1 Introduction

There may be a number of barriers preventing the development of tourism. Economic instability, lack of funding, socio-cultural dogmas, environmental and political unrest, terrorism, civil wars, high crime rates, etc. are common factors that act as barriers to tourism development. Inadequate transportation, communication networks, and essential services such as water and electricity, among others, hinder the development of tourism in any region. The lack of necessary infrastructure for tourism also acts as a barrier for the local community to participate in the tourism industry.

Limited private and public sector investments in tourism can constrain the construction of essential facilities and attractions. On the other hand, resistance from local communities to tourism development, fear of losing cultural identity, and negative effects on local traditions and the environment are different aspects that raise high concern for tourism development.

4.2 Barriers to tourism development

In **Table 4.1**, the identification of the barriers and the scores on the statements reflect the local community's perspectives and the hurdles faced by them while conducting business operations or entering tourism and allied businesses. The participants were asked to rate their agreement or disagreement with 20 different statements on a 5-point Likert scale.

The scale ranges from 1 to strongly disagree, 2 to disagree, 3 to neither agree nor disagree, 4 to agree, and 5 to strongly agree. As we have seen different dimensions of barriers to tourism development, this segment captures the existing barriers to tourism development in the study region and identifies challenging areas in running tourism businesses through the lens of a local community perspective on all four parameters of barriers to tourism development, i.e., infrastructural, operational, personal, and socio-economic (Yaja, M., 2021).

4.2.1 Infrastructural barriers

Infrastructural barriers in tourism are hurdles or limits in infrastructure that prevent the development and growth of the tourism business in a certain area. These barriers may include insufficient transportation networks, restricted lodging alternatives, bad road conditions, insufficient waste management, and a lack of amenities such as restaurants, stores, and recreational facilities.

In **Table 4.1,** in the category of **Infrastructural barriers,** the statement "Poor transportation network" acts as the prime barrier for tourism in the region, with (M = 3.88, SD = .988) with 51.8% of the respondents agreeing to the statement, as shown in Table 4.1. This is followed by "Inadequate telecommunication facilities" (M = 3.80, SD =.878), with 56.3% of respondents strongly agreeing with the statement. "Lack of sanitation & restrooms in public places" scored (M = 3.71, SD =.953), with 48.7% agreeing with the statement. Likewise, "Lack of Route Maps & Road Signs" and "Insufficient ATM & Banking Facilities" with (M = 3.66, SD = 1.019) and (M = 3.57, SD = 1.075), respectively.

4.2.2 Operational barriers

Operational barriers in tourism are any hurdles or challenges that limit the smooth functioning of tourism businesses, attractions, or services. These hurdles can be internal or external, and they may result from a variety of factors, such as communication inefficiencies, a lack of resources, inadequate infrastructure, language difficulties, cultural differences, or regulatory issues.

Under **Operational Barriers in Table 4.1**, "Lack of trained workforce for tourism" is rated as the major area of concern (M = 3.83, SD = 1.005), with 50.1% agreeing and 24.5% strongly agreeing to the statement. This is followed by "Lack of promotion about tourism job opportunities," scoring (M = 3.81, SD = .851), with 50.8% strongly agreeing.

Table 4.1 Respondents' views on Barriers to Tourism in the region

N=421	M*1	SD*2	SD %	D %	N %	A %	SA %
Infrastructural barriers							
Poor transportation network	**3.88**	.988	3.6	7.4	11.9	**51.8**	25.4
Inadequate telecommunication facilities	3.80	. 878	1.9	1.4	8.6	31.8	**56.3**
Lack of sanitation & rest rooms in public places	3.71	.953	3.3	7.1	23.0	**48.7**	17.8
Lack of route maps & road Signs	3.66	1.019	5.2	6.7	23.0	**46.8**	18.3
Insufficient ATM & Banking facilities	3.57	1.075	7.6	8.1	18.8	**51.1**	14.5
Operational barriers							
Lack of trained workforce in the region for tourism	**3.83**	1.005	2.4	11.6	11.4	**50.1**	24.5
Lack of promotion about tourism job opportunities	3.81	.851	.2	4.8	12.8	31.4	**50.8**
Low level of marketing & promotion of tourist places	3.69	.931	2.4	4.8	34.9	**37.3**	20.7
Lack of support from government	3.55	.996	.7	15.0	**33.0**	31.4	20.0
Lack of awareness about tourism as profession in the region	3.48	.903	.7	6.9	3.3	16.4	**72.7**

Personal barriers						
Lack of professional skills in Tourism	**3.83**	1.005	2.4	11.6	11.4	**50.1**	24.5
Lack of Education	3.55	1.003	1.7	17.6	20.4	**45.1**	15.2
Lack of financial backup	3.32	1.036	3.8	21.9	22.8	**42.0**	9.5
My opinion is not included in tourism planning	2.94	.820	3.3	29.2	**41.4**	23.2	3.0
Encouragement from family member is less	1.47	.903	**72.7**	16.4	3.3	6.9	.7
Socio-cultural barriers						
Strikes and bandh calls**a in the region	**3.60**	. 928	4.3	8.8	19.2	**58.4**	9.3
Leadership for tourism is less amongst locals	2.95	1.187	17.6	16.2	24.0	**38.2**	4.0
Lack of Support & Coordination from locals	1.72	.879	**50.8**	31.4	12.8	4.8	.2
Community is not ready for tourism development	1.71	.798	4.9	**42.0**	36.8	14.7	1.6
Local Culture not Conducive for tourism	1.61	.851	**56.3**	31.8	8.6	1.4	1.9

Source: Yaja, M. (2021) Community participation in tourism a case study of Arunachal Pradesh

Note: SD= Strongly Disagree, D= Disagree, N=Neither Agree nor Disagree, A=Agree, SD= Strongly Agree; M*[1]=Mean, SD*[2]= Standard Deviation.
Higher Means indicate a higher intensity of barriers.
a- A Bandh call means a temporary block or shutting down of vehicle movements due to social or political issues.

37.3% of respondents agreed with the statement "Low level of Marketing & Promotion of tourist places" (M = 3.69, SD = 931). The statement "Lack of Support from Government" scored (M = 3.55, SD =.996), with 33% opting for a neutral opinion. However, the statement "Lack of awareness about tourism as a profession in the region" scored (M = 3.48, SD =.903); 72.7% strongly agree with the statement.

4.2.3 Personal barriers

Personal barriers in tourism businesses are individual limitations or psychological variables which restrict or impede persons from participating in tourism-related business. These hurdles might be internal or external and include lack of confidence, language barriers, cultural differences, lack of education, lack of professional skills, socioeconomic constraints and other such issues.

The personal barriers parameter from **Table 4.1,** the statement "Lack of professional skills in tourism," in the **Personal Barriers** category scored highest (M = 3.83, SD = 1.005), with 50.1% agreeing and 24.5% strongly agreeing to it, which is followed by the statement "Lack of Education" (M = 3.32, SD = 1.036). "Lack of financial backup" scored (M = 3.32, SD = 1.036), with 42% agreeing to the statement. "My opinion is not included in tourism planning" scored with (M = 2.94, SD =.820) 41.4% opting for the neutral option. The statement "Encouragement from family members is less" remained the lowest among all statements (M = 1.47, SD =.903); 72.7% strongly disagreed with the statement.

4.2.4 Socio-cultural barriers

Socio-cultural barriers in tourism develop due to variations in social and cultural norms between tourists and the local community they visit. However, in this study, the author is only focusing on the supply side; the demand side's (tourist) opinion will be covered in another book. Socio-cultural barriers, especially in rural parts of tourism destinations, may take many forms, including language, norms, cultural restrictions, etc. when entering tourism and allied businesses.

Table 4.1 provides various statements related to socio-cultural aspects. The statement, "Strikes and bandh calls in the region" scored highest in **Socio-cultural barriers** (M = 3.60, SD =.928), which is followed by "Leadership for tourism is less amongst locals" (M = 2.95, SD = 1.187). While other variables under socio-cultural barrier scored lesser Mean; "Lack of Support & Coordination from Locals" scored (M = 1.72, SD =.879) with 50.8% strongly disagreeing with it, and "Community is not ready for tourism development" scored (M = 1.71, SD =.879) with 42% disagreeing with it. The state for the "Local culture is not conducive for tourism" is the lowest under the socio-cultural barrier (M = 1.61, SD =.851), with 56.3% strongly disagreeing with the statement.

It is evident that the growth of tourism in the study area faces several challenges, the majority of which are region-specific barriers. We have classified these barriers into four categories: infrastructural barriers, operational barriers, personal barriers, and socio-cultural barriers. However, some other forms of barriers may be specific to a region or country, depending on the level of tourism development.

For instance, the poor transportation network received the highest score, closely followed by inadequate telecommunication facilities in the list of infrastructural barriers. Similarly, the lack of a trained workforce in tourism as a profession is followed by the lack of promotion of tourism job opportunities under the segment of operational barriers. The lack of professional skills in tourism is followed by a lack of education from personal barriers, and finally, from socio-cultural barriers, strikes and calls scored the highest as barriers, followed by the lack of leadership for tourism in the region. Later sections of the book will discuss the recommendations and suggestions based on these findings.

4.3 Unique challenges of local community participation in tourism development

Even after India's independence in 1947, many parts of north-eastern India continue to remain behind, particularly in terms of real infrastructure development and the integral role of local people in the developmental project. These hamper the overall growth of the local community and also severely handicap them from engaging in tourism and allied businesses due to a lack of infrastructure facilities, such as a road network, transport, sanitation facilities, etc.

As such, the literature continues to echo the same infrastructural issue for example, Ziipao (2018) mentioned that the lack of necessary connectivity and infrastructure in northeast India is a major issue for indigenous villages. The lag in project development under India's Act East Policy is more pronounced in the region than elsewhere (Bajpaee & Bajpaee, 2017). Such a slow pace of development aggravates the situation and naturally hampers development, let alone tourism development. The Central Government's 'Act East' policy was proposed in the early 1990s. Decades have passed, and the project has undergone various changes during that time. Still, the project is struggling to take off in full swing in many regions, though some projects have started to see real progress in very recent times.

In this study, efforts have been made to understand the local community and the barriers to participation concerning the tourism business through personal interviews to gather perspectives and bring out a systematic identification of the barriers. This book aims to gain a deeper understanding of the issues that significantly hinder the local community's participation. The researcher asked open-ended questions to explore and understand several possible barriers in the four distinctive categories: infrastructure barrier, operational barrier, personal barrier, and socio-cultural barrier (Yaja, M., 2021).

The comments from respondents are:

"Our road condition is the most difficult and hurdle for visitors in the region. ***If the road became better, everything would fall on the right track, and tourism could be in full swing.*** *Right now, the mobile network connection is terrible, and it reduces our customers for the region."* (Tour Operator, Respondent no.295)

"The current condition of ***roads is extremely poor*** *and acts as a barrier for tourism.* ***Government should focus on sustainable tourism, should involve local youths.*** *I feel our youth also need motivation. Need waste management in the region.* ***Local food and brewages should be promoted instead of importing from outside."***
(Homestay owner, Respondent no. 172)

"Network problems are a significant barrier here, and our ***business works only with a reference and word of mouth. Our guest is our brand ambassadors."*** (Homestay owner, Respondent no. 264)

"The ***mobile networks do not operate properly*** *here, and our location is very far from town; thus, we are getting fewer tourists. We* ***cannot depend only on tourism;*** *on off seasons, we work with Border Roads Organization (BRO) as a daily laborer."* (Homestay Service providers, Respondent no. 99, 100 & 101)

According to service providers, the lack of telecommunication facilities is a significant barrier to tourism. This may be a regional barrier due to topography and landscape. Respondents' comments also reflect problems with the region's basic civic facilities, such as a lack of sanitation and other related concerns. Many respondents highlight transportation-related barriers as a major concern. As we can observe, from the comment of respondents nos. 208 and 295 express concerns about the lack of good air connectivity, irregular electricity supply (Resp. no. 52), the high cost of transportation etc., in the region.

A shortage of professionally trained and qualified human resources in tourism is a major operational barrier. The region's tourism industry is still in its early stages of growth. Locals are still unfamiliar with tourism opportunities and requirements. Furthermore, the few locals involved in the tourism industry have limited knowledge and information and rely on trial-and-error methods. Operational barriers are inextricably related to other variables that lead to overall tourism barriers. A pro-tourism development policy by the concerned authority changes the operation of businesses in the destination and lowers the barriers to participation in tourism for the local community (Goodwin, 2002; Neto, 2003). In the case of the study area for tourism policy, Arunachal Pradesh's concern authority for tourism development, namely the Directorate of Tourism in the state, is still in the process of drafting its tourism policy. This was found during the survey for the study. However, the local community, which is interested in tourism and allied services, was hopeful about their guidance and good initiative in this regard.

Concerns related to personal barriers: Many respondents confessed that they lack technical skills and language barriers (Resp. nos. 284 and 293), as a result of which they are not able to participate in tourism activities with full potential. These results are in line with the study by Su et al. (2019), where the authors also found a lack of expertise with the right skills is a barrier to participation tourism business. Responses in the present study related to personal barriers are also in line with the quantitative findings of the study. Systematic training and commitment to overall capacity building for tourism professionals in the region are paramount. Some of the comments are:

> *"I prefer domestic tourists due to the language compatible with them."* (Hotel Manager, Respondent no. 284)

> *"There are **no lifts/elevators** in most hotels in the regions, which acts as **barriers for elders tourists** and to those who required them. Even if we installed a lift, it would be challenging, especially during winter as **electricity is not regular**. Our government should provide regular electricity."*
> (Caretaker of a Hotel, Respondent no. 52)

The research did not find clear signs of resistance from the local community or society's elders, and as such, socio-cultural factors were not among the top scores among the parameters tested. These infer that there are no obstacles to tourism growth in the area on the socio-cultural front. However, the socio-cultural findings contrast with those of other studies on rural destinations, as Sood et al. (2017) found that socio-cultural factors hindered locals' participation in tourism and acted as a major barrier.

> *"...**the politician of the state are promoting tourism in such a way that people have high expectations from destinations of the region, but in reality, it is challenging to meet the expectation due to the low level of infrastructure and poor road conditions** of the state. And some locals do not understand the working nature of tourism, and sometimes they are not friendly to the tourists. If the state wants to promote the tourism industry, there should be massive **mobilization from the ground level**, from village to high-level authority."* (Tour Operator, Respondent no. 211)

> *"**Lack of promotion and not able to target the right audience** are important barriers apart from general infrastructure barriers. Local communities should participate more in tourism-related awareness camps and training. The local **participant should be encouraged to promote themselves** on various social media platforms to reach audiences. And our state is not yet ready for the tourism industry in full-fledged due to many barriers, and lots of groundwork is required at the grassroots level."* (Tour Operator, Respondent no. 208)

The findings of the present study are a one-of-a-kind example of how first-generation local community members participate in the tourism industry without any socio-cultural dogmas. However, the region suffers from other barriers, especially poor infrastructural facilities and more active leadership for the tourism industry, which are also highlighted in comments by tourism service providers. Some of the observations of respondents are given below:

> *"I am comfortable with Hindi. I generally do not keep foreign tourists; it is not that I do not want to keep them; it is **because of my language barrier** and as I have to report to local police about their stay. I run the business alone, and most of the staff are ladies. For us, it is challenging to deal with such issues. And to avoid these, sometimes I excuse tourists, by saying that --no vacant room available, for which I feel bad later and as I am **also losing***

> *"**Leadership is less in the communities for tourism**. We find it difficult to hire locals and sometimes they are not regular on work, mostly they tend to be absent for their work in the village. We need an employee who can be here in the hotel on duty on time."* (A hotel Manager, Respondent no. 47)

From the above observations, it is evident that there is a gap in job channelization in the region, despite the many guide training programs conducted by the tourism department. Ironically, none of the participants in the guide training programs are listed as guides on the official portal of tourism (comment of respondent no. 201). This is further supported by many respondents' views that there is no good representation of local talent in the tourism sector in the region. There is an urgent need to step up awareness camps in the rural areas of the region. All local youth who are interested can participate without having to worry about traveling to the city for mandatory training programs.

4.4 Summary

Chapter four explained the common barriers to tourism growth and the difficulties local communities encounter while participating in the process of tourism development. Four main types of barriers to tourism development have been talked about in detail: infrastructural barriers, which include physical and logistical problems; operational barriers, which include the practical problems that come up during tourism operations, such as bureaucratic problems, complicated rules, and operational limitations; and personal barriers, which are the beliefs, attitudes, and behaviours of individuals that affect tourism growth.

Lastly, socio-cultural barriers explain how cultural differences and social dynamics might hinder the growth of tourism, impacting both residents and tourists. While the research did not find significant sociocultural resistance among study participants, the chapter also highlighted the distinct challenges that local communities face when participating in tourism development. Addressing these challenges is necessary to ensure proper local community involvement, empowerment, and the preservation of local culture and identity in the face of changing tourism trends.

5. Integration of Locals
and Tourism Development

CHAPTER 5
INTEGRATION OF LOCALS AND TOURISM DEVELOPMENT

<u>Learning Outcomes</u>

The chapter provides collaboration and integration among tourism stakeholders, the role of local communities in tourism development, and the significance of capacity-building programs in fostering inclusive and sustainable tourism practices. After reading the chapter, you will be able to understand:

- the integration of tourism service providers for overall growth of tourism
- the significance of involving local communities in the process of tourism development
- the role of capacity-building programs in promoting an inclusive approach to tourism, the local
- the necessary skills and knowledge for communities to be equipped with for tourism development.
- The local community needs support systems to actively engage in tourism-related activities.

5.1 Introduction

Empowering local populations is a critical component of responsible and sustainable tourism development. Integration of local communities in decision-making is one of the first things a local authority can do to nurture and prepare locals for tourism development in any destination. These approaches can strengthen local communities, enhance their standard of living, and guarantee the tourism sector's long-term prosperity. The locals' participation is essential in determining their requirements, goals, and issues associated with the development of the tourism industry in a new or proposed destination.

By involving them, one may encourage a sense of pride and accountability for the results of tourism amongst community members. Capacity-building programs can scale up local communities' professional tactics, like strategic business operations, upskilling and reskilling training programs, and effective marketing and promotion of tourism products and services. Skills like digital marketing, building an online presence, and working with tour guides and travel companies are part of the capacity building that is necessary to stay profitable in the market.

5.2 Integration of tourism service providers

To assess the perceived integration of local tourism service providers, responses were obtained through statements, as shown in **Table 5.1.** These statements were created considering the level of integration of local tourism service providers in the design and development of tourism products and services in the region.

Table 5.1 Respondents' views on integration in tourism development

N=421 Statement	Mean	Std. Deviation	SD %	D %	N %	A %	SA
Involvement of local population in developing tourism products	2.85	1.018	10.1	**34.9**	22.1	28.6	4.4
Outside agencies have taken up tourism projects in the region	2.81	.839	4.4	**37.6**	35.1	20.7	2.2
Tourism projects in the region are fairly distributed	2.71	.798	4.9	**42.0**	36.8	14.7	1.6
Awareness of the various tourism development schemes in the state	2.63	1.038	6.9	**56.5**	5.9	28.7	2.1

Source: Yaja, M. (2021) Community participation in tourism a case study of Arunachal Pradesh

Note: SD= Strongly Disagree, D= Disagree, N=Neither Agree nor Disagree, A=Agree, SD= Strongly Agree. Higher Mean indicated higher agreement with the statements.

As little as one-fourth of the respondents were positive towards the involvement of local people in the development of tourism products, while 35% of respondents disagreed with the statement. About 38% of the respondents disagreed with the view that outside agencies have taken over the tourism projects of the region, while in close proximity, 35% of the respondents opted for neutrality on the same statement. 42% of the respondents were of the view that the development of tourism products is not fairly distributed between external and local agencies. It is, therefore,unfortunate that the majority of the respondents (56.5%) were not aware of the development of the region with respect to tourism projects and the various schemes included for tourism development.

When respondents were asked whether they feel outside agencies have taken up tourism projects in the region, the result showed a mixed view **(Table 5.1)**, with around 38% disagreeing, 35% opting for neutral, and only 20% still agreeing with the statement. The results depict that some local people are not included or are not involved much in the tourism development process.

With regard to the fair distribution of tourism projects in the region, 42.0% of the respondents disagreed with the statement "Tourism projects in the region are fairly distributed," and 37% (36.8) were neutral. This shows that respondents perceive that tourism projects in the region are not fairly distributed. And it shows that they do not have a clear idea or are not aware of project distribution in the region. The majority of respondents believed that the involvement of the local community in the decision-making process for the implementation of tourism projects in the region was minimal, and they were of the opinion that tourism projects in the region were taken up by outside agencies.

5.3 Integration of locals in tourism development: Extracted through open-ended questions

We've observed that responses to various statements tend to be mixed most of the time. For instance, when it comes to the distribution of tourism projects in the state, a significant number of respondents (42%) hold an equal opinion, whereas roughly 37% hold a neutral stance. This suggests that some respondents may be uncertain about the benefits or may not be aware of the available tourism schemes. Therefore, to enhance the study's depth and comprehensiveness, the researcher gathered additional responses by asking open-ended questions related to the statement presented in **Table 5.1**.

Some of the statements from respondents are:

*"**Transport service opportunities always go to outsiders**, and tourist hires taxi/cab from Guwahati for the entire trip in Arunachal in that scenario we are not getting any transport service from tourist here. **We should channelize local transportation system efficiently and properly.**"* (Homestay owner, Respondent no. 295)

*"Locals can take the best decision as whatever tourist attraction is available is the intangible asset of the local, but they **need some help from the government and an expert** who are in the industry for a sustainable."* (Tour Operator, Respondent no. 168)

*"Whenever projects come, planning should carry out only after **consultation with village elders** and local resource persons for better integration; Projects should not directly be given to outside experts; this process should always go hand in hand."* (Homestay owner,

*"**Transportation is generally hired from Guwahati, and they book it for the entire trip**, and here locals are missing out on the opportunities."* (Transport Service, Respondent no. 235)

"Everything is difficult in the transport business, locals need sensitization about human behavior, and we are not treated well by customers. Income from this business is very negligible and challenging to survive just on it. ... It's difficult to depend on this business to run the family." (Transport Service, Respondent no. 252)

"There is a conflict in the transport business; Guwahati acts as the entry point to Arunachal Pradesh; it gives people of Assam a better transport service opportunity as many tourist groups hire taxis/ book cabs for the whole tour package. And, tours last for 5 to 15 days, in such case only accommodation and food business is going to local service providers." (A hotel Manager, Respondent no. 221)

"While initiation for any tourism project, there should be proper consultation from all stakeholders. They should implement policy with proper consultation and successful stories while integrating local resources and cultural diversity." (Tour Operator, Respondent no. 177)

"I do not know about the schemes and promotions; only a few people who are in touch with the department must be knowing them well. Department should inform elders in the village about upcoming tourism projects without informing them there will not be a healthy start." (Homestay owner, Respondent no. 311)

"We need to promote our culture and nature as key USPs of the state to the right audiences. The benefit of tourism is not delivered to locals, and I strongly feel that we really need to do something about this." (Tour Operator, Respondent no. 209)

> *" ..If we observe our ancestor's way of living, it was sustainable and friendly to the environment.* We should bring back those values and integrate them through tourism in the region. So that it preserves and saves the unique practices of our ancestors." (Tour Operator, Respondent no. 210)

> *"I have observed that tourists are looking for small items.* So we need to cater to that. Our *handicrafts should be promoted as a souvenir for tourists;* we have beautiful crafts available and all these features can be a part of tourism." (Homestay owner, Respondent no. 300)

> *"Any project in the region should be well informed to locals, and the department should be should bring success stories of similar destinations like Sikkim. **It can be challenging to include everybody's decision, but some consultation with locals should be initiated.** For that reason, an expert should have broad perspectives in the project where all get benefits from tourism."* (Homestay owner, Respondent no. 86)

> *"**Locals should produce more products needed for tourism.** Hotel and resorts should use local resources for tourism. **The folk dance participants should be given a monthly salary for the same,** if they are called to perform. Hoteliers can make even this payment in the region from their revenue. This creates extra income/revenue for locals and also promotes local culture."* (Guide, Respondent no.185)

We can infer from the respondents' comments that we should encourage the local community to participate in forums or meetings and also make necessary rules for profitable business operations during the tourism development plan in order to increase awareness of tourism development in their area. For instance, organizations from outside the region provide many of the transportation services for tourists in the area, demonstrating the need for the authorities to enhance local transportation services and develop a stronger business ecosystem in the area.

The incorporation of community perspectives, as expressed in various forums, gatherings, and other events, may help to understand the opinions of the local community. These views could be utilized as inputs in the decision-making process and to monitor the delivery of services. It is essential to include members of the community in the deliberation and decision-making processes about the expansion of tourism. The growth of the local community is often hindered by a lack of information and awareness; nevertheless, the participation of the local community in various tourism development initiatives can assist the gap between stakeholders and decrease barriers.

The general well-being of the community in the area can be improved by implementing programs that increase awareness of the potential benefits of tourism. The socio-cultural environment of the state of Arunachal Pradesh is quite unique and diverse, and it has rich natural resources, including a wide variety of flora and fauna. If these resources are directed in the appropriate manner, they have the potential to become an essential source of economic livelihood (Yaja, M., 2021). This will, in the long run, lead to the production of economic value for rural people in the state.

5.4 Capacity building programme and inclusive approach for tourism development

To understand the inclusiveness of local tourism service providers in the various capacity-building programs and supports for tourism development, see **Table 5.2.** The results demonstrate the need for massive groundwork for capacity building and training programs for tourism service providers in the region.

Table 5.2 Capacity building programme and inclusive approach

N-421	Respondents who opted "YES."	Percent	Respondents who opted "NO"	Percent
Did you attend any meeting or public discussion forum related to tourism?	217	51.5	204	48.5
Did you receive any training/capacity building program to manage tourism services?	168	39.9	253	60.1
Did you receive any financial assistance for a tourism project/business?	99	23.5	322	76.5

Source: Yaja, M. (2021) Community participation in tourism a case study of Arunachal Pradesh

As can be seen in Table 5.2, roughly half of the people who responded to the survey took part in the meetings or talks that were held to address the growth of tourism in the region. A little less than one-quarter of those who responded had even been offered financial support through one of the many tourism development programs that are available. Roughly 40% had some sort of training in the field of tourism service operation.

As we have already seen, there is a lack of awareness or knowledge about the region's tourism plans within the local community, which hinders residents' integration into the entire tourism development process. Another factor could be that they attend less or do not attend any public meetings or events linked to tourism development, which makes the locals have such perceptions.

5.5 Support system for local community

Capacity building at the local level, such as providing hands-on training in tourism-related services to local youth, is regarded as critical to improving service quality. According to Stem et al. (2003), appropriate teaching and increasing awareness in a campaign manner help maintain long-term sustainable tourism and help communities. Timothy (1999) conducted a study in Indonesia and found that entrepreneurship training programs in the English language, accounting, hygiene and housekeeping services, guesthouse management, and business potential in food companies had a beneficial impact on their businesses. Some locals are apprehensive about communicating with international guests due to the language barrier. These constraints impede business participation. However, all these issues are solvable with adequate awareness initiatives and capacity building.

Here are some comments from respondents related to capacity building:

"Locals do not have awareness about how it can be promoted and the potential of their resources. For these reasons, they need an expert to help them out. Local also should be corporate for the development. Locals do not involve much in tourism, very few understand and participate in this profession." (Tourist Guide, Respondent no. 185 and186)

"Our tour guide and professional need better trainings and exposer. We need strong leadership in this profession. Our youth can create lots of opportunities in this line, rather than looking for jobs outside." (Hotel Owner, Respondent no. 301)

"Our society should be encouraging more. Need more involvement, we know about our culture and local resources. We need some expert assistance for greater exposer. Many of our youth are unemployed here, and few are going out to other cities in the country in search of a job. Our youth should be trained in this profession to be able to get a job and serve our state. I have observed many outsiders are taking up the job." (Hotel Owner, Respondent no. 198)

"Many of us never attended any training in tourism and did not have much business idea about it. But two of our members have attended such programs." (Transport Service, Respondent no. 334-343)

"Locals here do not understand the value of tourism, and it is potential for development. Therefore, Govt. should give us training so that we can perform better in the job." (Transport Service, Respondent no. 234-235

"Since 2004, I am in this industry, and I found there is no proper marketing for the destination. I have many areas to points out in barriers to tourism in the region. Some of them are:-

i. *The involvement of locals is less in my observation; most of the human resource personnel in accommodation units are from Assam.*

ii. *There is a logistic problem in the state, especially in the transport system for tourists.*

iii. *There is No tourism board / Corporation in the state. Whereas other states like Sikkim and Himachal have a corporation, every work related to tourism is systematic.*

iv. *Helicopter service within the state should be made available; there was no single domestic airport, but one started very recently at Pasighat. The first* **commercial flight commenced on 21st May 2018. We lose many tourists because we do not have airports to connect with the rest of India and International.**

v. *The politician of the state are promoting tourism in such a way that people have high expectations from destinations of the region, but in reality, it is challenging to meet the expectation due to the low level of infrastructure and poor road conditions of the state. And some locals do not understand the working nature of tourism, and sometimes they are not friendly to the tourists. If the state wants to promote the tourism industry, there should be massive mobilization from the ground level, from village to high-level authority."* (Tour Operator, Respondent no. 211)

"The **telecommunication do not work in the remote locations and remain days and sometimes for months** *without telecommunication. There are challenges in online payment system in remote locations due to poor coverage of internet; as a result only cash payment works here and* **many tourists find it challenging as they are habitual to online payment mode.** *Sometimes, we need to give cash to our guests(tourists) for onward travel expense as there are No ATM in remote regions. Hoping to get it back after they return their home destination.* **Only trust and hope work here…."** (Hotel Manager, Respondent no. 226)

Providing the needed skills and awareness about the opportunities encourages the locals to participate vigorously in tourism business activities. The native culture and tradition could be promoted as unique tourism products, apart from bestowing appreciation and acknowledgement of the local culture and Indigenous products and services. In many parts of the world, the social transformation of rural areas due to tourism and related sectors is commendable, with minimal negative impacts on the destination when carefully regulated.

The process of integration involves many marginalized groups in economic activities while advancing the lives of participants. Without proper training, knowledge, and participation from individuals in the tourism industry, the business may not be suitable, and its performance may not be satisfactory. Launching capacity-building initiatives and motivating locals can address these issues. Furthermore, knowledge of the positive impact of tourism reduces negative perceptions and acts as a catalyst for tourism development in tourism destinations.

Capacity-building benefits include, first and foremost, serving as a platform for addressing ground-level challenges and providing communities with an international perspective. Second, it reduces leakage. The development of indigenous human capital and the positioning of local resources in the system. As a result, capacity building also opens up opportunities for the multiplier effect of the economy within the social circle.

5.6 Community participation in tourism beyond livelihood

The nature of tourism participation, particularly among rural people, is influenced by a variety of socio-cultural elements. Participation in tourism and allied businesses establishes a mechanism to track tourism's social, economic, and environmental effects on communities. This information can identify potential problems, and planners can use the information for developmental strategies that can be changed accordingly, investment in initiatives and organizing capacity-building training programs for tourism development. Such capacity building can cover topics like sustainable practices, guiding, hospitality, and other related skills that can improve the standard of tourism services.

The promotion of the preservation of culture and heritage is one of the critical factors, which goes beyond livelihood opportunities. It is rather the preservation, presentation, and conservation of local culture. These include local culture, traditions, and heritage, which are also promoted as essential components of the tourism experience. For example, through storytelling sessions, heritage walks, cultural festivals, and museums, tourists can learn more about the way of life in their new surroundings.

Infrastructure and other public facilities improve the overall tourism experience; therefore, upgrading local infrastructure and facilities becomes a necessary requirement. This includes making investments in infrastructure, sanitization, healthcare, and other necessities that benefit both visitors and locals. Promote economic connections between the tourism industry and regional companies like the food, handicrafts, and agriculture sectors. These activities will create greater connections and lead to a snowball effect, bringing in economic benefits and opening jobs for other allied industries.

5.7 Summary

Chapter five provided the concept of integration in the tourism industry that involves the local community as the tourism service provider. The cooperative endeavours, alliances, and interactions among different groups involved in providing tourism services are discussed. This is accomplished by analyzing the answers received from open-ended questions, which allows readers to understand the qualitative investigation of how the local community is included in wider tourism development efforts.

The later parts of the chapter examined how community-based programs that focus on improving skills and knowledge contribute to tourism development in both an inclusive and sustainable way. It considers several aspects, including social, economic, and cultural support systems that contribute to the general well-being of the local community. In the following chapter, we will learn how local tourism service providers market their tourism products and services, as well as the challenges they face in the process.

6. Marketing of Community Tourism Products and Services

CHAPTER 6
MARKETING OF COMMUNITY TOURISM PRODUCTS AND SERVICES

<u>Learning Outcomes</u>

This chapter provides information on the marketing and nature of rural tourism products and services. Rural tourism products and services comprise several activities that encourage and support tourism in rural areas, enabling tourists to immerse themselves in and interact with the local culture, nature, and community. These activities enhance visitors' experiences with diverse products and services, including homestays, farm stays, local culinary, farming, participating in fairs and festivals, and many facets of rural lifestyle. And after reading the chapter, you will be able to understand:

- Local community tourism products and services
- the nature of marketing with respect to community-based tourism products and services
- marketing techniques being used to promote community tourism
- how local communities build partnerships with stakeholders to enhance marketing and branding.

6.1 Introduction

Rural tourism aims to strengthen local economies and safeguard community heritage by advocating for sustainable tourism practices. Most of the time, rural tourism products and services prioritize sustainable tourism, advocating for environmental preservation and community advancement. By advocating for rural tourism, communities can reap the advantages of enhanced economic prospects and a broader range of visitors.

Community service providers mostly find it difficult to do marketing and promotional activities, which is why most of these service providers rely on third-party stakeholders to sell and advertise their products and services. To phrase it another way, local tourism services are integrated into the larger market pool and made available to clients by third-party groups. Thus, commercial tour operators, guides, and government agencies sell local tourism services to customers. Therefore, it is important to explore why such cases happen and to understand the characteristics of local tourism products and services.

6.2 Medium of assistance for tourism services and marketing

Marketing plays a vital role in connecting with both existing and potential customers and also in maintaining competitiveness in the fast-paced tourism market. Any business firm's marketing strategy determines its long-term existence in the market and provides parameters to check its performance (Yaja, M., 2021). Therefore, the following items, which are given in **Table 6.1**, were asked in order to gain an understanding of and identify the form of help for marketing their services from government officials, consultation with professional consultants, or purely depending on themselves.

Table 6.1 Mode of assistance for creation of tourism services and marketing

N=421	Self %	Through consultant %	Government official %
Designs of tourism Products	81	6.9	12.1
Fixation of the price	80.8	4.9	14.3
Marketing of products/ services	84.6	5.5	9.9

Source: Yaja, M. (2021) Community participation in tourism a case study of Arunachal Pradesh.

From **Table 6.1**, we can see that more than eighty per cent of the participants developed and designed the services, fixed the price, and marketed their products and services by themselves. Only 12% and 7% of them seek assistance from government officials and consultants to design or create products and services, respectively. When it comes to determining the prices of tourism products and services, only 14% of respondents seek advice from government authorities, while only 5% of service providers seek guidance from consultants. In a similar manner, only 10% and 5% of them seek assistance from government officials and consultants in marketing their products and services, respectively. These results amply indicate that service providers themselves take full charge of their products from the design stage to marketing, which is quite laudable. It is heartening to note that, by and large, they don't depend on intermediaries.

6.3 Branding of native/indigenous tourism products and services

Branding is an essential part of developing and administering a distinct brand identity for any firm. It holds significance for various reasons; for example, building a unique identity in a crowded market of tourism is often a challenge for the local community to establish themselves.

Table 6.2 result shows branding and marketing elements that reflect the features of local tourism products and services. The results show that 62.5% of respondents agree to not having a brand name in their services; this is added by 97.7% and 91.9% confirming that they do not have a sales target or marketing strategy, respectively, in the region. The results depict that most tourism services in the region are missing contemporary brand-building features.

Table 6.2 Branding features of tourism products and services

N-421	Yes %	No %
Brand/logo for tourism product or services	37.5	**62.5**
Presence of sales targets	2.9	**97.1**
Formulation of any marketing strategy	8.1	**91.9**
Alliance with other agencies for marketing of services	**73.2**	26.8
Priority for tourists interests while designing products and services	**85.3**	14.7

Source: Yaja, M. (2021) Community participation in tourism a case study of Arunachal Pradesh

In the case of keeping alliances with other agencies for marketing of services, it scored 73.2% for yes, and priority for tourist interests while designing products and services also scored 85.3% for yes, and it is the highest score from the yes segment, indicating service providers are doing well in these segments.

The branding of any business sets it apart from competitors and highlights a unique feature or represents its unique way of delivering tourism products or services, leading to recognition for your business. For example, a specific logo, the nature of the service, the company's distinctive message, the dress code, the nature of the marketing style, etc., can all serve as indicators of any brand.

We have observed that contemporary brand-building features that are very important for destination branding are missing in the region. The possible reasons for lagging in branding and unstructured business operations are that the tourism industry in the region is still in its early stages, the majority of tourism entrepreneurs belong to the first generation, and there is a lack of educational collaboration in tourism-related subjects.

6.4 Medium of marketing channel

Marketing channels are the many means or platforms used to promote a product, service, or brand to prospective buyers. These channels can be both online and offline and include strategies like social media marketing, email marketing, search engine optimization (SEO), pay-per-click (PPC) advertising, content marketing, influencer marketing, and others.

Table 6.3 Medium of marketing channels used by community tourism service providers

N=421	Yes %	No %
Social media	56.3	43.7
Word-of-mouth	55.8	44.2

Television ads	2.9	97.1
Billboards & Hoardings	1.9	98.1

Source: Yaja, M. (2021) Community participation in tourism a case study of Arunachal Pradesh

Table 6.3 lists the marketing channels that the local community uses to advertise its products and services. Over 50% of the firms use social media, while 55.8% rely on word of mouth to market their tourism services. Only 2.9% make use of television ads, and 1.9% use billboards and hoardings as their marketing channels. Social media and word-of-mouth promotion are important mediums for marketing in the region.

Television ads and outdoor advertising, such as billboards, are mostly costly, and all service providers in the region are microscale service providers. This compels them to choose more practical ways. It is evident that the majority of service providers rely heavily on word-of-mouth and more convenient methods via social media. These approaches are more individualized and have the potential to shape more client relationships. The digital shift also impacted the increasing prevalence of mobile phone usage in rural regions. Many enterprises, particularly small ones, are redirecting their attention towards cost-effective and easier ways of marketing on social media.

6.5 Frequency of promotion for tourism services

The frequency of promotion refers to the number or frequency of advertisements in marketing. It is a vital part of marketing strategy as it contributes to the maintenance of customer trust and loyalty and attracts new customers. Common frequencies of promotions include daily, weekly, monthly, quarterly, and yearly promotions. During the pilot study of this study, it was observed that the frequency of promotions was extremely low; for that reason, the final study was measured on a yearly basis rather than monthly or weekly, as presented in **Table 6.4.**

Table 6.4 Frequency of promotion in a year

N -421	Frequency	Percent
0-2 times	381	**90.5**
3-6 times	19	4.5
7 times and more	21	5.0
Total	**421**	**100.0**

Source: Yaja, M. (2021) Community participation in tourism a case study of Arunachal Pradesh

The frequency of promotion and marketing of products and services by the community in this study is presented in **Table 6. 4**. We can see that 90.5% of service providers promote their products 0–2 times, 4.5% do promotion just 3-6 times, and only 5% indulge in promotion 7 times or more in a year. It may be inferred from the data that most of the local tourism service providers are not actively marketing their services. To remain visible in the market, service providers need to promote their products and services more frequently and also connect with third-party agencies for a broader reach and to maximize profits.

6.6 Respondents' comments on the marketing of tourism products and services

To broaden the possible opportunity to collect more responses related to marketing patterns by the local tourism firms, open-ended questions were also asked. Their comments also resonate with the quantitative results that we have seen in this chapter. Some of them are:

> *"Our state is virgin in tourism, and we need to work on policy and sensitization to locals on tourism. Try to use maximum local resources. We **need to aim for sustainability in this industry** and should target responsible tourism practices. This **idea should be incorporated while marketing the destination. We need to understand our target audiences rather than mass tourism.**"* (Tour Operator, Respondent no. 208)

> *"Since I am mostly occupied with household tasks and **I am not an internet person, tourists come from referrals and word-of-mouth**. I get a lot of new clients from satisfied and happy customers. Internet and mobile network is not good in our village. In this situation, **former customers are my only hope for new customers.**"*
> (Homestay, Respondent no. 306)

And the respondents' comments give us more insights into the trends in the marketing of tourism resources in the region. Some respondents showed concerns about the need for diversifying tourism activities, increasing local awareness, and prioritizing responsible tourism. The respondents support a deliberate, sustainable, and fully integrated tourism development strategy that aims to attract responsible tourists while safeguarding the region's resources and cultural authenticity (Respondent Nos. 208).

Respondent highlights the difficulties of running a rural business with little availability of internet resources and a heavy dependence on word-of-mouth advertising (Resp. no. 306). A strong internet connection enhances service providers' online visibility and enables them to establish connections with prospective clients. On the other hand, without the internet and telecommunications, there is a significant barrier to using online platforms for marketing, customer engagement, and even online financial transactions. The statement also emphasizes the significance of trust-based transactions when conventional financial services are not available. The respondent advocates for enhanced comprehension and effective guidance from local authorities to encourage community participation in tourism development.

6.7 Marketing of community tourism products and services

As we have seen, word-of-mouth advertising and social media were the most successful forms of marketing. It is worth noting that in the region, word-of-mouth advertising is still a trusted and effective medium. However, tourism service providers' promotional activities were found to be low. As a result, many of the local tourism businesses are not able to integrate with the larger business system.

Many tourism service providers exclusively conceptualize the products and services and price them on their own. At the same time, a few businesses follow the advice of government officials and consultants. Findings reveal that community tourism products and services lack integrated marketing, communication, and branding strategies. These are important for a competitive market in recent times and to catch up with trends.

6.7.1 Marketing patterns of local tourism firms for their tourism products and services are:

Finding 1- Heavy dependence on word-of-mouth promotion: Local tourism businesses are more likely to use social media in their marketing. However, word-of-mouth promotion is perceived as a trusted method of developing customer relationships and receiving referrals from local tourism firms. This finding is supported by the respondents' comments, which were presented earlier.

Local tourism businesses do place a higher value on word-of-mouth marketing, but they cannot rely solely on it. Because the trends are shifting, local tourism businesses must incorporate both WOM (word-of-mouth) and e-WOM (electronic word-of-mouth) into their marketing strategies. The gap or lag in marketing activities can be bridged by incorporating technology into word-of-mouth marketing.

Finding 2- Low promotional activities: Local tourism firms' promotional activities in the region are relatively low. This could explain why many service providers believe strongly in the value of word-of-mouth marketing, even though most service providers use social media for marketing, as evidenced by the interview excerpts. The reasons could be a variety of barriers, such as a lack of telecommunication facilities in remote villages, a lack of education, and other related issues.

Sharing destination experiences on social media creates business opportunities and influences customers' choices of destinations. Building a positive image of a tourist destination through social media is a trend in the market. Local community tourism businesses may use social media as a strategic tool for increasing exposure, reaping the benefits of their business, and achieving their full potential.

Finding 3- Self-reliance in curating tourism products and services: Most tourism businesses in the region conceptualize their own goods and services. The interview revealed that several service providers had previously been tourists before launching their businesses outside the state. They learned about the idea and conceptualized their services from their previous experiences as guests in other destinations. Furthermore, as previously mentioned, service providers' marketing and promotion are mostly done through various conventional methods.

Finding 4- Lack of strategic marketing plans: Most local tourism services in the area lack strategies related to market targeting, branding, and integrated marketing communication, which are key elements of an overall marketing strategy.

6.8 Key elements to consider while marketing local tourism products and services

Figure 6.1 presents primary elements to consider when creating marketing plans for any tourism products and services. Most local tourism service providers collaborate with other tourism businesses in the area to generate business leads and improve their visibility.

Tourist preferences are taken into consideration by the region's tourism companies, and service providers are trying to keep up with the trends, even though they lag in other marketing segments.

Figure 6.1 Marketing of tourism products and services

Elements to consider while marketing & promotion
✓ Keep tourists' interests in mind while designing tourism products and services. ✓ Keep a brand logo or tagline that represents your product or services or your business unit. ✓ Keep decent sales targets. ✓ Create a marketing plan and strategy. ✓ Alliance/collaborate with other agencies for marketing ✓ Keep the price of products or services slightly higher or lower than the average in your area or penetration pricing if your business is new.

Marketing channels	
✓ Social media ✓ Word-of-mouth ✓ Television ads ✓ Billboards & Hoardings	Frequency of promotion can be done on the capacity of the service providers either self or through consultants

For better operational convenience and positioning of the community-produced tourism services, they need social media's support to increase brand awareness. In this case, understanding the scope and nature of services will help authorities curate necessary training programs and help businesses take the right steps. Another important element is integrated marketing, which is a key aspect of any enterprise. Service providers must incorporate numerous integrated marketing tools to promote community tourism services.

Community tourism firms operate on the basis of referrals from consumers who have visited them, used their services, and then recommended them to other potential customers (Yaja & Kumar, 2021). In other words, extensive use of word-of-mouth promotion as a trusted medium. The visibility of tourism services, their strategic marketing, and how other potential customers interpret previous customers' testimonies will determine their success or failure. It is more prevalent in rural regions where there is not very much affluence on social media and people are not very active. The effectiveness of tourism marketing depends on the visibility of products and services among netizens as well as through the personal contact of influence groups.

6.9 Common characteristic features of local community-produced tourism products and services

To conclude the chapter, common characteristic features of local community-produced tourism products and services are listed. **These are.**

i. Highly unstructured products or services in terms of designs, price, and marketing patterns.

ii. Most of the tourism products or services are curated and designed locally without much assistance from any other source.

iii.   Do not represent well with the brand or logo for tourism products or services.

iv.   There are no sales targets in the business operation.

v.   No or less marketing strategy for products and services

vi.   High informal alliance with other agencies for the marketing of services.

vii.   High priority for tourist interests while designing products and services

viii.   Mostly trust and rely on word-of-mouth promotion.

ix.   More use of social media than television advertising for promotion.

x.   Minimal use of billboards & hoardings for marketing and promotion.

xi.   Promotion activities are relatively low.

xii.   No or minimal aggressive promotional campaign theme or message.

6.10 Summary

In this chapter, we have seen how and what marketing patterns are being practised by the community. The chapter discussed the support system, strategies for promoting tourism services, and marketing approaches employed by the local community. This includes the various types of assistance offered to improve and promote tourism services.

The chapter also included the community's viewpoints on the efficacy and difficulties of marketing, offering significant insights into the real-life experiences of their participation in the tourism sector. The last segment of the chapter offered the characteristic features of local community products and services. In the following chapter, we will learn how local tourism service providers interact with tourists and the professional experience in the business operation.

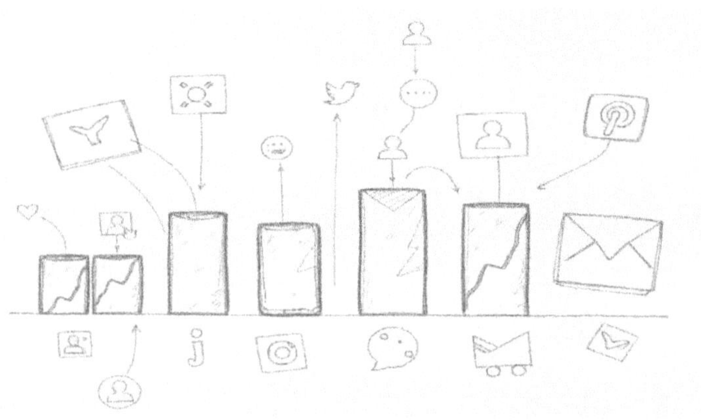

7. Professional Experience of Local Community

CHAPTER 7
PROFESSIONAL EXPERIENCE OF LOCAL SERVICE PROVIDERS

Learning Outcomes

This chapter describes the local community's experience running a tourism business. Professional experience in business refers to the skills and knowledge earned while working in any business firm or organization. It may include skills and information acquired through formal training and instruction, as well as those obtained through hands-on experience and on-the-job training. A professional with extensive business experience usually has a thorough awareness of the industry and market trends and the capacity to assess and solve complicated business issues. In this chapter, we will look at the experiences of local community service providers in the tourism sector. After reading the chapter, you will be able to understand:

- Professional Experience of the Local Tourism Service Providers
- Gain comprehensive knowledge of the roles and responsibilities of the tourism service professions in rural area

- Analyze and interpret the motivations and perspectives of individuals and communities seeking to engage in the tourism industry
- Service providers' opinions about tourism development in the state.

7.1. Introduction

Experienced service providers are more likely to have refined their abilities, be familiar with best practices, and comprehend how to cater to tourists' needs and preferences. This can result in increased customer satisfaction and favorable reviews, which can attract more visitors to destinations. For example, experienced local tourism service providers have in-depth knowledge of the destination, including hidden treasures, cultural insights, and lesser-visited attractions. This knowledge enables them to offer authentic, one-of-a-kind experiences that travellers may not discover on their own or through less-experienced providers. When local service providers have professional experience and a willing attitude toward service, the destination gains a positive reputation. They are also more likely to develop alliances that benefit both the firms involved and the customers they serve.

7.2 Experience in dealing with tourists

Tourism services demand professional expertise and confidence. Examples include providing guidance, arranging lodging and transportation, and other similar activities. Tourists are more likely to have faith in service providers with a track record of providing safe and satisfying experiences (Yaja, M., 2021). As we have seen in the earlier chapters, the study area is in the early stages of tourism development, and the service providers are also all first-generation. In this situation, it is an important stage to improve and correct necessary business operations to mold in the right directions that reduce negative impact and create maximum profit from tourism operations.

Tourism operations may be confronted with unforeseeable obstacles, such as weather disturbances, emergencies, or changes in travel plans. Getting opinions from those who are already working in this sector will open various challenges, concerns, and suggestions for further overall improvement of the tourism industry in the study and also in similar other destinations. **Tables 7.1 and 7.2** comprise items that highlight the professional experience of local tourism services, and how they feel and perceive their service.

To obtain the respondents' experience in dealing with tourists, two different statements are given on a 5-point Likert scale as shown in **Table 7.1.** The weight on the scale ranges from 1 to strongly disagree, 2 to disagree, 3 to neither agree nor disagree, 4 to agree and 5 to strongly agree. 56.1% of respondents strongly agreed with the statement "I feel happy and comfortable in dealing with tourists" (M =4.40, SD =.826), and 50.8% agreed with the statement "I feel Tourists are happy & satisfied with my services" (M = 4.26, SD =.978). The responses indicate that more than fifty per cent of the respondents are comfortable with interacting with tourists and feel that customers are happy with their services.

Table 7.1 Respondents' views on dealing with tourists

N-421 Statement	M	SD*	SD %	D %	N %	A %	SA %
I feel happy and comfortable in dealing with tourists.	4.40	.826	0	5.5	5.7	32.5	**56.3**
I feel Tourists are happy & satisfied with my services.	4.26	.978	3.1	4.3	6.7	35.2	**50.8**

Source: Yaja, M. (2021) Community participation in tourism a case study of Arunachal Pradesh. M=Mean, SD*= Standard Deviation.

7.3 Professional experience as a tourism service provider

In a similar passion, an attempt was made to obtain the satisfaction levels of the respondents in the tourism profession. The question includes job satisfaction and other issues associated with the professions, as shown in **Table 7.2**. Responses to the statement "I feel proud that I am associated with the Tourism Industry" scored (M = 4.30, SD =.984), with 56.3% of the respondents strongly agreeing with the statement.

Table 7.2 Respondents' views on professional experience as a tourism service provider

N-421 Statement	M	SD*	SD %	D %	N %	A %	SA %
I feel proud that I am associated with the Tourism Industry	4.30	.984	2.4	4.5	10.0	26.8	56.3
I encourage my friends and relatives also to participate in tourism business	4.17	1.113	4.0	6.9	10.0	26.6	52.5
I am willing to continue in this profession	4.01	1.222	4.8	13.3	5.5	29.0	47.5
I am satisfied with my engagement & participation in tourism	3.99	1.079	1.7	12.1	12.4	33.5	40.4
My business/job is steady & stable	3.96	1.128	3.1	10.7	14.7	29.7	41.8
My business/job is able to support myself and my family financially	3.51	1.359	7.4	25.2	29.3	25.9	32.3

Source: Yaja, M. (2021) Community participation in tourism a case study of Arunachal Pradesh. M=Mean, SD*= Standard Deviation.

The statement, "I encourage my friends and relatives to also participate in the tourism business," scored (M = 4.17, SD =

1.113), with 52.5% of the respondents strongly agreeing with the statement. The statement "I am willing to continue in this profession" scored (M = 4.01, SD = 1.222), with 47.5% strongly agreeing with the statement. The statement, "I am satisfied with my engagement & participation in tourism," scored (M = 3.99, SD = 1.079), with 40.4% strongly agreeing with the statement.

Responses to the statement "My business/job is steady & stable" scored (M = 3.96, SD = 1.128), with 41.8% strongly agreeing to the statement. However, only 3.1% of respondents still strongly disagreed with the same statement. This indicates some respondents have concerns that their business/job is not stable. And 14.7% of respondents were neutral, which implies they are unsure about the stability of their job or business in the future. The statement, "My business or job is able to support myself and my family," scored (M = 3.51, SD = 1.359), with 32.3% of respondents strongly disagreeing with the statement. At the same time, 9.3% of respondents were neutral about the given statement. And 7.4% of the respondents strongly disagreed with the statement.

More than fifty per cent of the respondents feel proud that they are associated with the tourism industry and are positive about encouraging their friends and relatives to participate in the tourism business. Many of the respondents agree that they are willing to continue in this profession and are satisfied with their participation. However, as we can observe, few respondents feel that the business or job is not stable and the income from the industry is not sufficient to support themselves and their families financially.

7.4 Respondents' views on opportunities to participate in the tourism industry

The service providers were asked an open-ended question to express their views on their experience and opinions for development in the tourism industry. The main aim of this approach is to obtain their honest opinions and document the experiences of local tourism service providers. Respondents' comments are illustrated in **Table 7.3.**

Table 7.3 Respondents' views on possible participation and opportunity in the tourism industry in Arunachal Pradesh

What are the possible ways, according to you, in which the local community can participate in the Tourism Industry?	
Comments	Opportunity for development/p articipation
"Guides are less during the season; there is ample opportunity in the accommodation sector also. We have a tie-up with the tour operators. During the season they contact us for the tourist service." (Hotel Manager, Respondent no. 05)	Guide and in accommodation sector

*"Local people should be involved in the tourism industry for alternative income even if they are working in other professions. For example, Tourists can be offered a farm visit (visit to paddy field, orchard, bamboo garden etc.) as they love to visit farm areas. The local community, especially those who are actively farming, needs to integrate with this profession to share a small share of income with them. We need to promote our culture and natural resources as key USPs of the state to right audiences. (*Tour Operator, Respondent no. 202)	Tourism as a source of alternative income for local farmers and other professionals.
"It is very difficult to get a local chef. There are lots of opportunities as a guide /chef. It is challenging to find a local chef. If we hire chefs from outside, they tend to alter tests as there is no written recipe or handbook; our traditional food making comes with practice, all knowledge has passed down through oral tradition. Some of our local people think that working in this profession is not credible, and they do not understand the value of tourism. And more importantly, our leaders have to understand the value of tourism for the region." (Homestay owner, Respondent no. 297)	Requirement of Chef with specialised in traditional cuisine and Guide
*"There are lots of opportunities in culinary. We are compelled to hire chef who are not trained in local cuisine, generally from outsiders, It's hard to find no local chef. One of our drawback is we do not have proper documentation on our food style and delicacies, as everything is pass down to us with oral tradition or by practically involving. We need to focus on this for the future generation We should retain our original food for authenticity. We should not imitate others culture." (*Tour Operator, Respondent no. 202)	Local Chef and requirement to document traditional ways of cooking
"It is challenging to find a guide most of the time. We are compelled to hire locals who have little knowledge about guiding tourists and who can deliver decent service. We even needed to approach school teachers as the guide for our clients. *"Tourist guides for culture and traditional dress are in*	Guide and Special local guide for cultural tourism

demand as tourists express interest to know them more. We also need nature guide. Most of the times taxi drivers act as a guide. And they, are not trained in the profession." (Hotel Owner, Respondent no. 01)	
"We should have more accommodation units because it is difficult to accommodate all of them during the peak season; when I tried to arrange them to neighbour house/ alternate arrangement, they do not feel like going there. So need more trained hospitality service providers in the regions." (Hotel Owner, Respondent no. 84)	Creation of more accommodation units
"The best guide is the local guide; our youth should be trained as a guide. We should build solid human resources from youth." (Tour Operator, Respondent no. 168)	Requirement of local tourist guides

Source: Yaja, M. (2021) Community participation in tourism a case study of Arunachal Pradesh

7.5 Respondents' suggestions for improvement in tourism development

To ascertain respondents' opinions about the tourism development in Arunachal Pradesh, service providers were asked to give their opinions on the areas that need attention from the directorate of tourism in the state. Being asked helps extract perceived opinions and an understanding of factors that require immediate attention for tourism development in the region. Respondents' views are presented in **Table 7.4.**

Table 7.4 Respondents' opinions about tourism development

Comment/opinion on area(s), Directorate of Tourism, Govt. of Arunachal Pradesh could focus on.	
Comments	**Focused area for improvement**
"Officials should travel more in the state's interior and remote locations rather than staying and focusing in Itanagar (capital city of Arunachal Pradesh). They need to know the ground reality. And training should be provided in the villages rather than in cities like homestay concept is for rural areas and how villagers will come to cities. For villagers, it is challenging to travel, and they cannot afford it. The government should take emphasis on skill-building." (Hotel Manager, Respondent no. 06)	-Seeking focused in rural areas from concerned officials -training and capacity building
"Passes (Permits) should be made an easy	-Sensitization about tourism for

process for the tourists. Copy of the same should also be sent in the state's check posts where police personnel can quickly check and save time." (A hotel Manager, Respondent no. 54)	personnel at check gates
"We need more coordination from both government and local villagers. The government needs to give more awareness campaigns about tourism to villagers. We needed to do a village tour for our tourists and for this reason villagers should also work for this. *Government and reviewers, especially private websites, should clearly message our facilities and give tourists a clear message as they read some information and expect those services. In a homestay, we could only provide whatever we have at our hands."* (Homestay owner, Respondent no. 111)	- Coordination between locals and government -proper review of the services in various online portal/website
"Most of our youth need to be motivated; I have observed those who did a Tourism and Hospitality course and look for another government Job elsewhere after a few years of working in the industry. There should be proper channelization of job and job security in this line. Every year,	- Creation of jobs through Tourism - list of local guides on the official tourism pages and websites

Department of Tourism in the state conducts training programs for guide. But none of them have been registered themselves and listed on the tourism website of Arunachal Pradesh." (Tour Operator, Respondent no.201)	
"Every youth is running for a government job here or go out in metro cities of other Indian states, and there is so much competition. I feel the government should create some alternatives jobs through tourism in the region." (Hotel manager, Respondent no. 294)	-Creation of jobs through Tourism - Creation of jobs will reduce youth migration
"...here, locals do not understand the value of tourism; therefore, they are missing out on many golden opportunities. Arunachal Pradesh is such a wonderful state in term of its culture and topography. The state is blessed with a unique natural gift. Most of the locals do not understand the power and potential of their resources." (Tour Operator, Respondent no. 211)	-Sensitization about tourism industry for locals - preservation of culture and tradition
"Our people require sensitization programs on tourism even if they are not associate with tourism to understand its pros and cons." (Tour Operator, Respondent no.219).	- Sensitization about tourism industry for locals

"The department should focus on local people's sensitization about tourism and its working style. It should also be imparted to all locals' concerned sectors/departments related to tourism, like transport sector and various outlets eateries. Department is not focusing on the right audience. It is my honest opinion. The concept of Atithi Devo Bhawa should be instigated in every mind of residents of the state, not only tourism professionals. Then only tourism can grow here in a sustainable way. *People here do not understand the importance of traditional value and their culture through tourism angles. They need to promote this through tourism."* (Hotel manager, Respondent no. 228)	- Sensitization about tourism industry for locals -focus on the right audience for tourism promotion -preservation of culture and tradition
"Government should provide us some basic training for communication with tourists. We do not have enough parking place. There should be sufficient space for parking, and it should be maintained well. Authority should check and inspect in between over it is management. Government should work on infrastructure building in the regions." (Transport	- Training for communication skills -infrastructure for tourism and parking spaces in tourist sites

Service, Respondent no. 135-145)	
"Police personnel in the check gate should be trained well, as sometimes they are rude to tourists while checking for passes in the check post. They should be a little sensitive to tourists. There should be a separate team/ police personnel for tourists in the check post." (Tour Operator, Respondent no. 177)	-Sensitization of police personnel in check gates about tourism and tourists
"Still, we have no tourism board or Tourism Policy in the state. We need to create a tourism policy in the state, and it is still on frame and consideration." (Tour Operator, Respondent no. 202)	-Emphasised on Tourism Policy/ tourism board in the state
"Our tourist information should be updated on the official website of tourism. Many of the information and photos need an update. Sometimes, tourists feel cheating if they do not find the same in the destination. Need more publicity and promotion of the destinations. Specific promotion for the destination. e.g., like adventure destinations, monastery sites, agriculture tourism should be the emphasis." (Homestay owner, Respondent	-Updating information about tourism on websites -promotion of destination Specifications

no. 306)	
"The department should work in consultation with local people, as we know what we can offer and what not in the industry. And our villager needs to be given the right ideas to generate income in the line." (Homestay owner, Respondent no. 315)	-Integration of locals -convey the right information for benefits from tourism development
"The department does not know much about the resources we have; we have to work together to develop. The department should instigate us to work more and motivate it for better participation. Before any initiative, they should consult us, as ultimately whatever effect will come to us." (Guide, Respondent no.327)	- Integration of locals - consultation and information with locals for tourism initiatives in their locality
"There can be one window system for accessing permits. Currently, in check gate police forces are deployed, officers can be trained for handling tourists. There is a need of sensitization for all concerned departments related to this hospitality and tourism industry. This permit should be handy and easy to cater all groups of tourist, many elders those who are not that	-Easy access of permits -trained personnel at check gates - proper maintenance of the tourist sites - connectivity as a barrier for tourism

ease with technology handling are missing out, they do not want to hassle in this process, therefore they choose another state in the region, which do not has such permit is for this, this also gives some kind second thought/work as a barrier to visiting the state. And clean and proper maintenance of the tourist sites, cities and towns is need of the hour. Most tourist places are in dilapidated conditions. *Connectivity in the region is the major hindrance for tourism in the state. More awareness camps in the villages and remote level as villagers cannot go to towns and cities. People from cities know more about tourism, our villages need to know it more." (*Transport Service, Respondent no. 330)	- awareness and campaign about tourism in villages
"Government should develop better infrastructure and service in the existing tourist circuits. First, Primary investment should be made wisely. As there are many imprecise investments made by departments like building circuit houses in remote places and where tourists do not go, and no one lives, and is not in a good condition. As a result, the cattle and other animals are	-Better infrastructure for tourism -timely maintenance of existing tourism facilities

making it their home. Second, Good roads and proper mobile network coverage.'' (Homestay owner, Respondent no. 86)	
"Our government needs to tap the potential for other areas like- Religious tourism, Buddhist study site of the state should come under the Buddhist circuit of India, in Tawang we have India's largest monastery and second largest in the world after Tibet Monastery; still, the Indian government does not cover that it is under Buddhist circuit map of India. *Another issue is cleaning the surrounding, which we can manage, but the government has to provide other necessary infrastructure to run the business.* *There is no regular taxi service in the town. We homestay owners have to arrange them.* *We have a cleaning drive camp once every week, and I am currently in charge of our colony.''* (Homestay owner, Respondent no. 262)	- Promotion of destination based on its specific/uniqueness -cleaning of tourist sites - seeks necessary infrastructure for tourism businesses
"Government should focus on the maintenance of tourist spots, and there should be some more activities for tourists	- Maintenance of tourist sites - seeks more

so that they can stay some more days in the region. We receive different types of tourists; for this reason, there should be different activities to cater to them. We need bigger support for them. Need more support from the department, like giving training to local youth. The government has built some circuits house, but nobody is there to manage and run them for the tourist." (Guide, Respondent no. 192)	support from the department(tourism)
"Our government should promote our state to in the right target audience and in the proper channels." (Tour Operator, Respondent no. 201)	-Promotion of tourism to right audience
"There should be specific destination promotions about its specialties like segregation of tourist interest, religious site, Monastery, trekking site, culture, wildlife, etc. (Tour Operator, Respondent no. 210)	- Specific destination promotions
"Update of tourist information on websites is urgent attention of the region. Many a times tourists follow the information given on the tourist website of the department. Photos and scenic are no longer like on the	- Updation of tourism information on websites

website, so all current images should be updated at least one year to reduce misconception. The images they are using are more than 10 years old." (Homestay owner, Respondent no. 320)	
"Our festivals should be promoted well, and they should be incorporated with a resident as these festivals happened in the local villages." (Guide, Respondent no. 326)	-Promotion of various festivals

Source: Yaja, M. (2021) Community participation in tourism a case study of Arunachal Pradesh

7.6 Interpretation of respondents' opinions on tourism development

In this section, we are going to draw inferences and perspectives from the comments gathered from the respondents. However, **Table 7.4** presents a concise interpretation of the comments under the specific area of focus. The study region can undertake numerous development and improvement initiatives to fully realize its tourism potential.

However, we will discuss some of the key points interpreted from the comments in this section, which deserve immediate attention. These highlighted points are important for development as well as improving existing services that need urgent attention from the concerned departments and stakeholders involved in tourism and allied services.

7.6.1 Awareness about tourism opportunities in remote/rural areas

Many respondents emphasized the need for aggressive campaigns to raise awareness about the natural and cultural resources for tourism development. Service providers in rural areas seek more attention and assistance from concerned officials to ensure the smooth operation of their businesses (comment of respondent no. 06). In addition to the awareness campaigns, respondents also expressed a need for training and capacity-building programs for tourism service providers. (Respondent No. 06, 135–145).

7.6.2 Sensitization of police personnel at check gates

The police personnel handling the tourists at the check gates for permits (tourist permits) should be given additional training to handle tourists. They need to be sensitized and trained in soft skills for dealing with tourists, as it is at these checkpoints, tourists gain their first impression of the culture and hospitality of the host community. A feeling that tourists are welcomed in the region needs to be created. (Respondent Nos. 177, 211, 219, 228, and 330).

7.6.3   Coordination of locals and government

The level of acceptance and tourism development is strongly interlinked with the socio-cultural and other resources of the destinations. Respondents expressed the need for coordination among residents and government agencies for service marketed and the kind of service available in the destination to create memorable experiences for tourists. (Respondent no. 111 & 192).

7.6.4 Authentic review of tourism services

These are the days of social media. Social media touches our lives day in and day out to the extent that perceptions are formed and influence the decision-making behavior of tourists. In this regard, online reviews play an important role in influencing customers. A homestay owner expressed concern about authentic reviews of services on various online platforms (Respondent No. 111). Authentic reviews help service providers identify the gaps in service delivery and improve upon them. Further, good reviews present the service in a positive manner and connect the guest with the hosts, leading to a win-win situation.

7.6.5 Targeting the right audience

Respondents expressed the need to promote tourism to the right audience (Respondent No. 228). Focusing on the right audience for promotional activities saves time and resources in meeting the objectives of the service firm.

7.6.6 Better Infrastructure for tourism operations

Infrastructure at a tourist destination plays an important role in successful business operations. The lack of infrastructure in the region was expressed by respondents (Respondent No. 086, 135–145, 330). Lack of adequate infrastructure as a significant barrier has also been identified from perceived barriers in the study's quantitative analysis.

7.6.7 Preservation of culture and tradition

Respondents expressed concern about local culture and traditions and the need for preservation (Respondent Nos. 211, 228, and 326). Similarly, the promotion of local culture and festivals was expressed (Respondent No. 326).

7.6.8. Emphasize the importance of tourism policy

There is a strong concern for the need for a tourism policy in the state. The need for tourism policy is expressed by a senior tour operator (Respondent No. 202).

7.6.9 Timely updates of information related to tourism

The importance and need for updating information about tourism on official websites were raised by respondents (Respondent Nos. 306 and 326).

7.6.10 Destination-specific tourism promotion

Many service providers emphasized the importance of promoting specific destinations' specialities (Respondents 210, 262, and 306). The region's diverse tourism resources may be marketed and promoted accordingly rather than promoting the whole region as a destination for a particular type of customer. Promoting each destination with its niche resources is a sure way to maximize diverse customers and customer retention.

7.6.11 Creation of jobs through tourism

Respondents suggest the government should create more jobs through tourism as the youth of the region are forced to migrate to other states in search of livelihoods, primarily to many cities and towns in other Indian states. (Respondent Nos. 201 and 294).

7.6.12 Easy access to permits

A respondent (Respondent No. 330) expressed the need for simple and tourist-friendly procedures for issuing permits. During the field study, it was found that the process was much easier for domestic tourists to obtain an e-ILP from the official website of Arunachal Tourism. One could also get a permit on arrival at Lokpriya Gopinath Bordolio International Airport, Guwahati, and Railway stations in

Assam and Arunachal Pradesh. However, a foreign tourist is required to apply for PAP only through registered tour operators and other concerned government authorities.

7.6.13 Proper maintenance of tourist sites

Proper maintenance of existing tourism facilities and upkeep of tourist sites were considered of paramount importance by the service providers (Respondent Nos. 086, 192, 262, and 330).

7.6.14 Integration of locals

The local service providers feel that the tourism department should work in close connection and integration with locals and the host community's views, as they (the locals) know what they can offer and what they cannot in the industry (Respondent Nos. 315 and 327). Respondents also expressed interest in providing villagers with appropriate ideas and motivation to enhance income generation and opportunities.

7.6.15 Documentation of traditional practices

The concern for traditional practices and documentation was also expressed (Respondent No. 202). Many young people lack knowledge about the ingredients and cooking methods used by our ancestors, potentially jeopardizing the preservation of traditional delicacies in the future. Other areas, such as cultural and traditional practices, also need documentation for future generations.

It is reasonable to interpret and conclude from the comments that there is an opportunity for locals to participate in tourism. Respondents perceived job opportunities in tourism, such as chef, guide, and accommodation services and the requirement to document traditional practices and ways of cooking in the region. In addition, some respondents consider tourism an alternative source of income. The local community can take measures to protect the environment, preserve cultural heritage, and assist the local community while developing any tourism product and service, thereby promoting responsible and sustainable tourism.

7.7 Summary

Chapter seven discussed the local community's professional experiences, attitudes, and opinions on the potential and challenges in tourism and allied businesses. We have observed the diverse participation of locals in the development of tourism. Gaining insight into the personal experiences of those local communities engaged in the tourism business is essential for fully grasping the practical aspects of business operations, helping the tourism planning authorities make the right decision, and making readers look through different perspectives.

Discussions from different viewpoints are essential for formulating ways to improve, contribute a qualitative aspect, and maximize the engagement of the local community in general. In the next chapter, we will explore various Self-Help Group (SHGs) and other independent associations participating in tourism development.

8. Self-Help Groups and Tourism Development

CHAPTER 8
SELF-HELP GROUPS AND TOURISM DEVELOPMENT

<u>Learning Outcomes</u>

This chapter introduces special interest groups in tourism development and their contribution to creating unique experiences for tourists, the inter-departmental association for tourism development. All these are primary data gathered during the field visits and observations made in various tourist destinations. After reading the chapter, you will be able to understand:

- special interest groups and their motivation for entering the tourism business
- tourism initiatives led by local communities in the tourism sector
- the significance of community participation in shaping tourism experiences
- introduction to the inter-departmental association for tourism development

8.1 Introduction

A self-help group (SGH) is a group of people who come together to support and assist one another in overcoming a specific problem or cause, consisting of common goals or interests. The aim of SGH can be anything, such as empowering women by improving their social and economic standing, promoting gender equality, and offering a platform for collective action. Including a self-help group is essential for a comprehensive interpretation of the data. It also helps with proper context and appropriately represents their participation in tourism development (Yaja, M., 2021).

A special interest group (SIG) is a community within a larger organization that shares a common interest in advancing a specific area of interest, knowledge, learning, or profession. Members collaborate to effect or produce solutions in their specific field, and they may communicate, meet, and organize conferences. By and large, these SGHs and SIGs focus on their specific interests or causes. The former mostly focuses on specific issues or challenges, and later on a common hobby, passion, or profession. In this chapter, we will focus on how these various groups are taking part in tourism development and their initiatives rather than on their individual entities.

8.2 The importance of local groups and tourism development

It is important to incorporate these opinions in tourism development, as they directly and indirectly affect tourism and tourism development. This inclusion is a way of acknowledging their contributions to the field and incorporating possible suggestions in tourism planning and development. For this study, several field visits were made to meet with resource persons and respondents to integrate the results of the qualitative data with the quantitative data. Important data from field surveys and observations are included in this report.

Field surveys are essential for collecting primary data directly from various stakeholders. It enables researchers to capture data in the field, allowing them to obtain accurate and current information. Researchers can adapt this primary data to meet their qualitative research objectives, and it is useful for comprehending specific contexts and phenomena. In this study, the field surveys help the researcher acquire a more in-depth understanding of the environment, culture, and distinctive characteristics of the study area from the ground. During the field surveys in this study, many independent groups, societies, and clubs were found engaging in tourism-related livelihood activities.

8.3 Arunachal Tourism Society

The Arunachal Tourism Society (ATS) is an initiative of the Directorate of Tourism, the Government of Arunachal, and other concerned departments of Arunachal Pradesh to promote tourism development in the state. ATS was registered on 15th Dec. 2016 under the Society Regd. Act. 1860 to guide and monitor the overall development of Tourism activities in Arunachal Pradesh. **It is a** developmental society for tourism and allied activities that includes all related government governing bodies and important stakeholders from the local community. The main objective of the society is to promote travel, tourism, leisure activities, and the management of tourism infrastructure in Arunachal Pradesh. ATS has an administrative governing body that includes officials and elected local members to carry out the planning and development of tourism in the state.

Governing bodies of the society ATS include:
i. Home Minister of Tourism – Chairman
ii. Secretary, Tourism – Secretary
iii. Director Tourism – Convener
iv. Head of Department, Travel and Tourism, Rajiv Gandhi Polytechnic College – Member
v. Director, Research – Member
vi. Dy. Secretary (Finance) – Member
vii. Director, Sports – Member
viii. Director, Urban Development – Member

Approved members of ATS at district level are:
i. Deputy Commissioner – Chairman
ii. District Tourism Officer – Member Secretary & Convener
iii. District, Sports Officer – Member
iv. District, Research officer – Member
v. District Art & Culture officer – Member
vi. Dy. Director, Urban Development – Member
vii. Zila Parishad Member (ZPM) – Member
viii. Divisional Forest Officer – Member
ix. Executive Engineer (EE) or Assistant Engineer (AE) – Member

Collaboration facilitates the exchange of resources, knowledge, and expertise, allowing concerned departments to leverage their experiences and resources more effectively. Every policy execution necessitates close cooperation between government bodies and local organizations. For example, the state of Arunachal Pradesh has rich flora and fauna, attracting many researchers, environmentalists, natural lovers, and tourists from around the world. It needs the close collaborative initiative of the forest department and the state tourism directorate. This collaborative work gives a better chance that policies or initiatives are customized to suit the specific requirements and conditions of the region for holistic development.

Many times, the livelihood of the local community and the tribal culture depend on the forest ecosystem, and their major portion of socio-economic activities depends on the forest land. On top of that, ecotourism and nature-based tourism activities greatly depend on abundant natural and cultural resources. Most of the time, such resources are integral to the cultural practices of the local community. For this very reason, the integration of ZPM and the District Art and Culture Officer is of great significance, as are the other members, directly and indirectly.

The activities of their coordination for tourism development may include the exchange of information, synchronization of security activities, and oversight of the preservation and protection of both cultural aspects of the region and preventive measures for over-tourism and the negative impact of tourism. All these conservation efforts necessitate a collaborative approach to establish and implement legislation and policies addressing concerns such as deforestation, climate change, culture, air and water pollution, and sustaining the rich and fragile belt of the Great Himalayas resources in the state.

8.4 Self-help groups and their initiatives in tourism development

During the field study between September 2018 and September 2019, the researcher found that some special interest groups were actively participating in tourism and related activities, which directly or indirectly contributed to tourism development in the state (Yaja, M., 2021). These groups were formed by the local women group, farmers, youths, tourism entrepreneurs, etc. These groups were kept in contact until August 2021 to keep up with the updates if there were any for compiling the final inputs. The groups include:

- Bugun tribe in Eagle's Nest Wildlife Sanctuary (ENWS),
- Hong Farmer Club in Hong Village,
- Ngunu Ziro Homestay Group,
- World Wide Fund (WWF) for Nature, at Thembang,and Zimithang,
- Welfare Association of Shyo Village (W.A.S.V)

8.4.1 Bugun Tribe of Singchung Village

Bugun Trabe in traditional attire.
Image credit: Voices of Rural India

It was discovered that members of the Bugun Tribe from Singchung Village were taking part in ecotourism operations at the Eaglenest Wildlife Sanctuary. In addition to patrolling in the forest, the activities include nature guides, birding guides, and adventure activities. As part of the Community Reserve Forest (CRF) effort, the state's forest service recruited a few youths from the Bugun community.

They were given training on nature guides, nature photography, and adventure tourism activities, which are essential requirements to accompany visitors of different kinds, from researchers to tourists, in the sanctuary. They are given a monthly salary from the department. Even though the Department of Forestry in the state is not primarily responsible for tourism-related activities, they have taken an impressive step in that direction

8.4.2 Hong Farmer Club

Members of Hong Farmer Club dressed in traditional attire

Tourists in Apatani traditional attire

Image Source: Tilling Yam (Namiir), Member, Hong Farmer Club, 2019

Hong Farmer Club is an all-female farmer from the Apatani Tribe, residents of Hong village, Ziro Valley, Lower Subansiri district. The group usually performs when Hotels, Homestays, tour guides, and tour operators approach them for special performances for tourist groups, where they showcase their culture, dances, folklore, songs, and prepare exotic tribal food. Tourist groups also get a chance to visit the agricultural fields and experience the traditional lifestyle of tribal culture. Hong

Farmer Club received appreciation from both local authorities and the central government of India. The farmer's club won several accolades for their initiatives in other social causes too.

8.4.3 Ngunu Ziro Homestay Group

Another such example is **Ngunu Ziro Homestay Group**, whose initial motive was to keep Ziro Valley clean and preserve the local culture, but later some of the members started running successful homestay services in the region. When 'Ngunu Ziro' is translated into English, it means 'Our Ziro' Ngunu meaning 'Us' or 'Our' in this context.

Members of Ngunu Ziro during jungle visit.
From left: Shri Koj Mama, Shri Pura Tama, Dr. Tage Kanno, and Shri Punyo Tatu.
Image credit: Koj Mama

Ngunu Ziro Homestay,
Shri Punyo Chada with his wife.

Image source: Author

Initially, six families from the group visited Sikkim in 2010 to experience the homestay concept at the cost of their own expenses. After that, members renovated their houses and made some changes to suit the tourist's needs, and gradually this group expanded homestay accommodation facilities. Here is an excerpt from an interview with a local of Ziro Valley and an active member, Ngunu Ziro.

"Our initial aim was to clean Ziro Valley, and preserve our culture, later on we heard of the homestay concept, and we liked the idea. Here we intended to promote our culture and preserve the same. Our motive was never a profit-making from this business in tourism. Still, our motto of running homestay within our group is clean and preserving culture, cleaning the region, and promoting awareness of the same. Our team has around 12 homestays; none of us promote it for running a business and commercialize it. For this reason, we do not have a board and name/brand it on social media. In our system, it works on a references." **– Shri Pura Tama, Member of Ngunu Ziro, 2019**

8.4.4 WWF's Homestay Initiative in Thembang and Zimithang

The World Wild Fund for Nature (WWF) started training locals for homestay service in Zimithang and Thembang of the state in 2007 and provided initial financial assistance for the villagers.

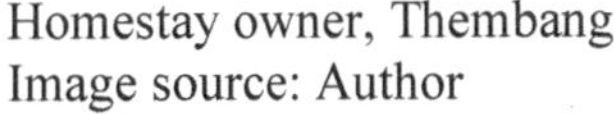

Homestay owner, Thembang
Image source: Author

Homestay owner, Zimithang.
Image source: Author

These selected villagers are trained in basic hospitality to serve tourists and to maintain hygiene while providing services. Officials also postulated *dos and don'ts* for tourists and homestay service providers. The comment of WWF's Project Manager is given below:

"In homestay, we distributed tables and dinner sets, as most of them were not having any such utilities. We kept the basic necessities for the tourists. Initially, our main objective was to conserve and protect the wildlife in the region though protection of red panda has given special emphasis in the region. Earlier, villagers were involved in the extraction of timber, hunting. We started to figure out what could be the socio-economic income for the locals. Our team did several surveys, like biodiversity survey, habitat survey in the region. We started a conservation organization that can involve

locals and also provides some means for livelihood. Then we identified tourism as a source of livelihood for the local community. We did a feasibility study of livelihood; tourism can be a sustainable approach for the locals, as the area is a bit rocky mountain, so for this reason, production from agriculture is also not possible. The area is unique for tourism. We made the team from the village consisting of Tent Manager, cook, pony men, porter, guide, etc. usually, this consisting of 10 -15 participant from villages."

-Project Manager, Mr. Pema Wanghe, WWF, 2019

8.4.5 Welfare Association of Shyo Village (WASV)

Tourists with Yak Dancers -Performing Artists from Shyo Village
Welfare Association
Image source: Author, 2019

The Welfare Association of Shyo Village is a unique initiative by youth from the Tawang district of the state. This welfare association organizes cultural shows especially, for tourists in Shyo Village, Tawang. The group consists of approximately 50 participants, most of whom were school students, unemployed youth, and farmers. This group obtains permission from the local authority to host the event for the tourists. A visitor can enjoy the program for just 100 rupees (Indian rupees), including three different local dances, tea and snacks, and a free dress trail for guests. The association made all these arrangements purely to keep tourists' interests in mind. A comment from a member, WASV:

"We do it every day; even for three visitors, we did it. So far, we have received maximum of guests of 200 in the evening. We start our program at 6 pm, and it lasts up to 8 pm, which is for two hours. We have received positive feedback so far from both visitors and local authorities. The age groups of our members, ranges between 15-40 years old, all our team members are local youths, who are students, farmers, unemployed youths, and youth who are searching for a job elsewhere." **(Member of WASV, 2019)**

Field surveys in this study offered contemporary data, allowing us to understand the present patterns, actions, and opinions of the local community participating in tourism development. The survey assisted in finding answers through the comments made by respondents about the connections between variables. This allowed making inferences based on empirical evidence from both quantitative and qualitative aspects with closed observation during the collection process.

This study's field surveys revealed these groups and their unique insights. The findings from field surveys offer the chance to investigate and discover some important aspects that were not previously considered for the study. For example, the initial objectives of this study were not intended for a self-help group. However, during the survey, it was found that these groups were actively involved in tourism and related businesses, which turned out to be significant enough to add these interest groups, SHGs and their initiative to the study. These field surveys played a vital role in making recommendations and suggestions, which we will discuss later in other chapters. This field survey will also guide future researchers in a similar context for longitudinal studies.

8.5 Summary

Chapter eight brought the contributions of special interest self-help groups in promoting tourism development and the initiative of inter-departmental collaborations. The chapter thoroughly examines the activities and efforts made by these groups to advance sustainable tourism practices and foster community involvement. The vital roles played by these SHGs in promoting sustainable practices and encouraging community engagement have been elucidated in this chapter.

These groups represent various endeavours, ranging from advocating for environmentally friendly accommodations to programs centred on protecting wildlife and supporting local farmers. The chapter also offered a broad analysis of the unique approaches employed by local communities for tourism development. Findings and observations from the field survey contributed significantly to the study's major objectives. It is pertinent to consider important elements and findings from field surveys in the case of qualitative studies to add suggestions and recommendations, which we will look into in the next two chapters.

9. Major Findings and Their Implications

CHAPTER 9
MAJOR FINDINGS AND THEIR IMPLICATIONS

Learning Outcomes

These major findings are significant results or discoveries from the study. The study presents these findings as its main takeaway or conclusion, incorporating innovative insights, new knowledge, and unexpected results. These findings could have significant implications for the tourism development research area or its key stakeholders. The goal of discussing these findings is to interpret and characterize the relevance of many results, comments, and observations made for the study. After reading the chapter, you will be able to understand the following:

- nature of participation in tourism services in the region
- popular tourism activities in the region
- identify challenges of community tourism service providers
- essential support systems required for smooth tourism development
- strategies and guidelines to address the shortcomings in the region's tourism support system
- importance of incorporating the perspectives and ideas of local tourism service providers in destination development.

9.1 Introduction

This chapter presents a summary of interpretations of significant research findings. The summary helps the readers find a reference point and understand where to find more detailed information on specific aspects of the research. The major findings are picked and considered to be revisited with attention and detail, which will be useful for researchers, practitioners, policymakers, academics, and anyone with a keen interest in tourism development.

The chapter highlights the aspects of research implications that are essential for discussing the major research findings, emphasizing their significance, and offering a roadmap for readers. It helps readers find relevant portions that were pointed out in the introduction, particularly in the literature review, and objectives in the initial chapters of the book. And thereby, a model for development and recommendations can be created from the research findings.

9.2 Highlights of major findings and their implications

The importance of highlighting significant and major research findings is crucial to conveying the necessary and actionable actions for the research objectives. This process lies in its ability to facilitate the communication of useful information to a broader audience, promote the sharing of knowledge and cooperative efforts for tourism development in the study area, and also relate to and apply to other similar destinations in India and other destinations in the world with similar challenges and opportunities for development in the domain of tourism and allied sectors.

By presenting these results, scholars can highlight new findings, encourage implications, and inspire opportunities for development. Furthermore, this can provide valuable insights for decision-making, stimulate innovation, and influence policy formation. Emphasizing significant findings also fosters responsibility by encouraging scholars to condense and document their findings, thereby promoting accountability and scientific integrity. Overall, this section aimed to facilitate research to have a more significant impact, benefit society, and expedite advancement among diverse stakeholders in the domain.

9.2.1 Participation of locals in tourism services

Participation in tourism the local community is found to be more active in the accommodations sector by owning and operating hotels and homestays. Less local participation in tour guiding has been observed, as also noted from the respondents' comments.

9.2.2 Nature of participation in tourism services in the region

Most tourism service providers in the region consider tourism services their primary occupation. It is important to note here that all the service providers are found to be first-generation participants in the tourism domain. Many service providers are from other professions, and they are participating in tourism services as a secondary occupation, creating an alternative source of income for themselves.

9.2.3 Existing tourism activities in the region

Current tourism activities are more focused on cultural, rural, and adventure tourism activities in the region. Action-oriented tourism activities leading to the upliftment of locals, like volunteering to teach in schools and communities, are minimal in the region. The suggestions for potential tourism activities for the region are given in the next chapter.

9.2.4 Region lacks basic support system for tourism development

The study found that the region lacks a primary support system for tourism development and needs assistance both from the state and the central government to take tourism to new heights in the region. Poor transportation networks act as the prime barrier to tourism development in the study area.

In addition, inadequate support systems for tourism, like poor infrastructure facilities and political disturbances, do play an adverse role in the development of tourism. Most of the places in the region are not accessible throughout the year due to poor transportation facilities. Many of the places worth visiting are inaccessible.

9.2.5 No visible cultural barriers to participating in the tourism profession

Although all the local tourism entrepreneurs are first-generation entrepreneurs in tourism services, they did not face any hurdles to entering the profession from family members. Further, the region's culture is also conducive to tourism development, as per the responses from the respondents. The community in the region faces no apparent sociocultural barriers to participating in tourism and allied businesses, which is uncommon in tribal communities. This shows the openness and progressive culture of the region.

9.2.6 Need for capacity-building programs in an inclusive approach

Most of the respondents confirmed that they lack professional skills in tourism. This hampers the overall development of tourism. Thus, the lack of a professionally trained workforce is a significant operational barrier in the region. The current service providers need basic training in service management and operational skills. For example, training in marketing and branding products and services to reach out to more customers. Such tourism services may be recognized and identified in the market by customers. There is also a lot of scope for jobs as guides and local chefs, which require special training and, most importantly, promote and include locals for these job opportunities.

9.2.7 Medium of assistance for service providers

It may be inferred from the comments of the respondents that the level of current assistance for tourism service providers from the government or concerned departments is not adequate. Simultaneously, curating tourism products and services is also solely the responsibility of service providers. One possible explanation for this is that most respondents have not been exposed to tourism training programs. Concerned tourism governing bodies must address this issue and implement training programs that are practical and destination-specific for local service providers.

9.2.8 Absence of branding in tourism products and services

Service providers were found lacking in business management skills and knowledge of branding and positioning their products and services. Service providers do not have sales targets and marketing strategies, which is reflected in the low frequency of promotion and marketing activities related to products and services. The majority of the current tourism services in the region do not have any brand identification. Most of the business is generated on a referral basis from old customers. It is found that 'Happy Customers' help these service providers contact new customers through word of mouth. Word-of-mouth promotion is a major component of the marketing activities of service providers.

9.2.9 Service providers' experience in the tourism profession

The majority of tourism service providers in the region are happy about their participation in tourism. It was also found that most service providers are comfortable dealing with tourists and are proud to be associated with the tourism industry. On a contrasting note, they are not satisfied with the income they are making from tourism ventures, and the responses amply made it clear that the income generated from tourism services is not sufficient to meet the basic needs of the family.

9.3 Action points and suggestions to integrate the local community in tourism development

It is found in the study that the integration of local communities in the tourism development process is less prevalent in the region. This could be one of the reasons why service providers are not aware of various tourism schemes and projects in the state. In this regard, the comments of the respondents are compiled, and points are illustrated for recommendation in the very next chapter.

In this segment, we will revisit and interpret the comments made by respondents during our interviews. These findings are unbiased extraction of the respondents that need attention from the concerned authorities to initiate the necessary steps and to create a better ecosystem for tourism development in the region. Following are the suggested action points.

Suggestions for the action points to integrate the local community:

i. Awareness and campaign about tourism in villages

ii. Training and capacity building programs

iii. Sensitization of police personnel at check gates

iv. Coordination of locals and government

v. Authentic review of tourism services

vi. Targeting the right audience

vii. Better infrastructure for tourism operations

viii. Preservation of culture and tradition

ix. Written documentation for local or traditional ways of cooking

x. Emphasis on the importance of tourism policy

xi. Updation of information related to tourism

xii. Destination-Specific Tourism Promotion

xiii. Creation of jobs through tourism

xiv. Easy access and standard regulations for tourist permits

xv. Proper maintenance of the tourist sites

xvi. Authentic representation of the destination in the tourism development

xvii. Integration of locals to reduce conflicts

9.3.1 Awareness and campaign about tourism in villages

Awareness and campaigns about tourism in villages would provide opportunities to understand and indicate the need for tourism development and entrepreneurial opportunities in rural areas. This will educate local communities about the potential and benefits of tourism and how it can be an additional source of income.

9.3.2 Training and capacity-building programs

Training and capacity-building programs emphasize the significance of training and restraining any skills required in hospitality, customer service, and other areas for efficiently dealing with tourists or visitors. For example, we have seen service providers in the region require training programs or develop skills to promote their tourism products and services. Further, some service providers did not receive any training programs.

9.3.3 Sensitization of police personnel at check gates

The sensitization of police personnel at check gates about tourism and various tourist types is significant, as they are the first people that any visitor or tourist meets while entering a new destination. Many visitors consider them the face of the state and a point where first impressions are built. These personnel are the face of the state in many ways.

Tourists may experience a shift in their mental state due to travel-related illnesses or may feel vulnerable simply because they are away from their home country. It is crucial to approach this situation with a certain level of sensitivity. Training is necessary to understand the unique needs of tourists. For example, these personnel must be trained in the soft skills necessary to enhance the touristic experience for visitors. Though this should not undermine the necessary verification and formalities, if the destination can manage to provide additional personnel, there should be one tourist police officer and additional regular personnel to maintain the balance for safety and security for both locals.

9.3.4 Coordination of locals and government

Effective coordination between local communities and government authorities is essential for the holistic development of the tourism industry. Coordination gives the opportunity to integrate opinions and minimizes confusion among parties. Multifaceted industries like tourism demand the involvement of all parties and require collaboration to plan, manage, and promote tourism in a manner that benefits all.

9.3.5 Authentic review of tourism services

Authentic reviews and feedback help service providers correct mistakes, make informed decisions, and improve the products and services. This is a significant way to maintain confidence in the business operation. This review may come from any inspection team, consultants, customers, etc.

9.3.6 Targeting the right audience

Targeting the right customers, or tourists, for rural tourism products and services gives service providers an added advantage. It is a fact that all tourists like to experiment and are ready to adapt themselves to rural tourism. Understanding the preferences and requirements of specific types of tourists can help to tailor marketing and service efforts.

9.3.7 Better infrastructure for tourism operations

A good tourism infrastructure helps increase the number of visitors, longer stays, and higher revenues for a destination. Additionally, it has the potential to generate employment opportunities and foster greater economic expansion in the region. However, the development plan should be holistic and aim for sustainable tourism.

9.3.8 Preservation of culture and tradition

While promoting tourism, it is essential to preserve the local distinctive culture and traditions. The local community members and its government must try their best to retain authentic characteristics of cultural value; thereby, tourism development should celebrate and highlight them.

9.3.9 Written documentation for cultural and traditional practices

The preservation of cultural heritage is one of the most crucial in the era of globalization and rapid cultural assimilation. The local traditions and culture in the study region were passed down to the next generation through oral tradition. Therefore, creating records and making proper documentation of traditional practices is a must to retain knowledge and maintain authenticity. For example, cooking methods are an integral part of a culture's identity.

And the written documentation helps preserve these culinary traditions, ensuring that they are passed down to future generations.

9.3.10 Emphasis on the importance of tourism policy

Tourism policy can play a significant role in shaping and managing the tourism industry for job regulation and the diversification of the economy. A well-crafted tourism policy can provide guidelines and regulations for development in a sustainable way and maximize economic benefits through better investment plans. The natural and cultural resources of the destination can be incorporated into tourism development with the help of policy. With the proper regulation, tourism products and services can also be introduced through sustainable practices that protect the environment, preserve cultural heritage, and benefit local communities.

9.3.11 Regular updates of information related to tourism

A regular update of tourism information, both online and offline, is essential for enhancing visitor experiences, ensuring safety, supporting business success, and promoting the sustainable development of destinations. This helps tourists plan their trips more effectively and allows tourism service providers to make informed decisions and adapt to changing circumstances. Timely information and updates help manage and protect fragile ecosystems and cultural heritage sites by implementing visitor limits, conservation measures, and responsible tourism practices.

9.3.12   Destination-specific tourism promotion

Destination-specific tourism promotion involves tailoring marketing and promotional strategies that highlight the unique selling proposition (USP) of a destination for the right audience. The primary goal of destination-specific tourism promotion should be to attract tourists to that specific destination by showcasing its unique and attractive features of culture and natural resources.

The promotional marketing theme and strategies can be customized for each destination type rather than the whole region. For example, the study area of Arunachal Pradesh has diverse tourism resources, both cultural and natural. These strategies may involve advertising, social media campaigns, content marketing, storytelling, and collaborations with travel agencies and influencers that focus on destination specific.

9.3.13   Creation of jobs through tourism

Tourism can be an important source of employment for local residents. The industry can have a substantial impact on employment by generating employment opportunities for locals through tourism-related activities. For example, accommodation, food and beverage units, transportation, tour operations and management, art and culture, marketing agencies, tourism boards, and tourism infrastructural development. The creation of jobs may reduce youth migration to rural areas.

9.3.14 Easy access and standard regulations for tourist permits

Simplifying the process of procuring tourist permits and other required documents can encourage more tourists to visit the state. Easy and well-regulated permits boost both the tourism industry and the local economy of a region. For example, easy access to tourist permits means more tourists spend money on tourism products and services, thereby creating more business opportunities for local SMEs like local tours, craft shops, artisans, and other allied service providers, which depend on the tourism industry for their livelihoods.

Well-regulated permits and hassle-free access to permits also track the movement of tourists and ensure their safety during any emergency or unforeseen situation, making it easier to locate and assist tourists. In addition, the regulation can assist in determining the carrying capacity for environmental protection in fragile destinations, ensuring a sustainable approach that does not harm the local environment or culture.

9.3.15 Proper maintenance of the tourist sites

Maintaining the sanitation, safety, and overall quality of tourist sites is essential for ensuring that visitors have a positive experience. For example, regular inspections for wear and tear, safety hazards, and environmental impacts make the site attractive. It also protects the local ecosystem by implementing sustainable practices, setting signs and cautions for safety measures, and placing an information board about the significance of the site.

The management team also must ensure that the site is accessible to all visitors, including those with disabilities. Implementing a feedback box for visitors, residents, and stakeholders to identify areas that need improvement and make necessary adjustments based on the suggestions makes any tourist site appear more appealing and gets maximum revisits.

9.3.16 Authentic representation of the destination in the tourism development

Involving local communities in tourism planning and decision-making promotes sustainable development. This preserves the destination's authenticity in terms of socio-cultural value and balances the economic benefits of tourism for locals. The locals have a genuine concern for their communities' long-term success and can provide valuable insights into how to preserve the natural and cultural resources in their region.

9.3.17 Integration of locals to reduce conflicts

This approach will mitigate potential conflicts, protests, and opposition to tourism development, and having them on the boards of planning can lead to more effective, coordinated, and sustainable development. Involving local communities in decision-making processes and giving them a voice in how tourism is administered can ensure that their needs and concerns are considered, resulting in tourism that is more sustainable and community friendly.

Therefore, the integration of locals helps anticipate and address these issues, fostering better relations between residents and visitors, which is important as many activities in the tourism industry have the potential to affect their lives and the environment. For example, locals feel a stronger sense of ownership and pride in their community for their culture and protection of flora and fauna. Being a tribal state, Arunachal Pradesh's culture is deeply rooted in natural resources, including their voices and concerns, which are crucial when developing any tourism planning and development. Collectively, these action points seek to promote responsible and sustainable tourism development in rural areas while preserving local culture and benefiting both the local community and tourists, as well as preserving the flora and fauna of the destination.

9.4 Observations and findings from the field surveys

Observations and recordings from field study visits are crucial for gathering firsthand data and insights into research. For this study, the author conducted several field visits in the five selected districts discussed in chapters one, two, and three earlier in the book. The observational points from this study suggest several areas for improvement in tourism development:

9.4.1 Need to diversify tourism activities

Government bodies and tourism activities are found to be concentrated on and obsessed with promoting ecotourism and adventure tourism. It may be due to the nature of the challenging terrain and mountainous ranges. However, they miss out on other potential areas like cultural tourism, agro-tourism, village tourism, pilgrimage tourism, educational tourism, and voluntourism activities that require immediate attention from the tourism board of the state and tourism service providers to diversify the tourism activities and extend the stay in the state.

9.4.2 Differences of opinion in income and nature of participation

 The respondents who are participating in tourism businesses primarily for livelihoods are not very happy with the region's current phase of tourism growth due to inconsistent tourist footfall and operational-related challenges. However, those who enter the tourism business out of passion or as a second profession are motivated and enthusiastic about their participation in the region's tourism activities.

9.4.3 Require maintaining tourism destinations and facilities

During the field survey, it was found that some tourist sites and government accommodation units lacked proper maintenance. Maintenance of tourist attractions is of utmost importance for many reasons. It shapes the initial impression, and it also plays a crucial role in ensuring tourist satisfaction. Furthermore, providing a hygienic and secure destination enhances tourists' experiences, increasing their likelihood to return and recommend the location to others, thereby supporting the country's tourism sector.

Tourist sites are frequently renowned landmarks destinations, and failing to maintain them can result in their deterioration and bad reputation, ultimately losing visitors further, leading to no revisit to the destination. Furthermore, well-managed tourism attractions have the potential to enhance local economies and generate employment opportunities, therefore making a valuable contribution to tourism development.

The field survey found that other stakeholders like local youth groups, interest groups, and allied departments like the Forest Department and WWF all did phenomenal work to scale up tourism development in the state. However, these stakeholders were not officially connected with the Directorate of Tourism. All these interest groups were found to be working independently on their own to assist local people directly or indirectly in the tourism business.

9.5 Summary

Chapter nine highlighted the scope and characteristics of community engagement in the tourism industry. The first few sections address common challenges, such as the need for a fundamental support system for tourism growth, highlighting the necessity of ground support systems for tourism development while also taking into account the local community of the tourist destination. The importance of capacity-building programs and an inclusive approach to empowering and involving the local community in the tourism industry were also included.

The major findings that need urgent attention were added under action points. The chapter concludes by presenting the field survey results, including valuable observations, and explaining how this qualitative aspect enhances the comprehensiveness of our knowledge regarding the socio-cultural and socio-economic linkages of tourism development. Furthermore, how these factors strengthen our understanding of the complex obstacles and potential for sustainable tourism development was also presented. The next chapter will be the concluding chapter of the book, in which we will see a model for tourism development.

10. Recommendations for Tourism Development

CHAPTER 10
RECOMMENDATIONS FOR TOURISM DEVELOPMENT

Learning Outcomes

This chapter presents recommendations and implications that stem from research outputs and remedies to specific problems based on findings. Research proposes recommendations for a course of action or solution to a problem, issue, or topic based on its objectives. The main aim of this chapter is to bring forward both qualitative and quantitative outcomes of analysis, interpretations, and observation. After reading the chapter, you will be able to understand:

- the importance of the tourism system and policies in destination

- assistance channels or help desks to support tourism stakeholders

- the required skills to design and implement training programs for tourism professionals

- the importance of special interest groups and their participation in tourism development.

- strategic planning and infrastructural development in the tourism sector is significant.

- the role of tourism policies is crucial in shaping the growth, monitoring, direction, and sustainability of the tourism industry

- model for community participation in tourism development that is recommended for tourism development.

10.1 Introduction

This chapter presents recommendations and implications based on the findings. The recommendations for implications are made and designed to provide guidance or direction to practitioners, policymakers, or other stakeholders. Recommendations can take numerous forms, including specific methods, policies, actions, or inspiration, and are usually based on the findings. The implications provided here are actionable, influencing future activities, policies, or interventions that we have read in the initial chapters of this book. It helps narrow down a large amount of information and direct attention to the important ones. The model and research findings may also be useful and can serve as a reference point for other destinations in developing countries and well-developed countries where the tourism industry has the potential to play a significant role in economic livelihood and development in all respects (Yaja, M., 2021). The chapter also included theoretical research contributions, implications, limitations, and suggestions for future research options for scholars interested in the subjects.

10.2 Recommendation for pro-tourism governance and pro-tourism systems in tourism destinations

Establishing a harmonious political environment and having a strong local government support system are critical factors for tourism development. Political instability and unrest hinder the progress of tourism initiatives by discouraging investors from investing in such ventures. There is a strong correlation between the government's interest in tourism and the overall evolution of the business environment, as well as the significance of power in this regard.

Pro-tourism government initiatives, such as visa-on-arrival and hassle-free visa processing, have made all of these possible. Tourism development frequently necessitates the improvement of infrastructure, such as transportation, communication networks, and utilities, which are primarily the responsibility of the government. A tourism-friendly administration can prioritize infrastructure development to improve the overall travel experience while also meeting the needs of the local population in this process.

Pro-tourism governance maximizes the positive effects of tourism on destinations and promotes sustainable tourism development. Tourism generates revenue, foreign currency, and employment opportunities, making it a significant contributor to economic development.

A tourism governance structure ensures that policies and strategies are designed to maximize economic gains and encourage industry investment. In order to reduce detrimental effects on ecosystems, fauna, and natural resources, pro-tourism governance emphasizes responsible tourism planning and management as a way to ensure such regional practices. Sustainable tourism practices are critical for preserving the natural environment and biodiversity.

Tourism is a labour-intensive industry, and pro-tourism governance can contribute to the creation of jobs in hospitality, transportation, retail, and cultural industries, among others. In many countries, community development is one of the primary objectives of tourism pro-governance. Tourism-friendly governance focuses on involving local communities in decision-making processes and empowering them to partake in tourism-related businesses. This can help reduce unemployment and enhance the destination's standard of living, thereby ensuring that residents receive a more equitable share of the benefits of tourism.

We must address issues such as setting up an airport, improving the road transportation system, and fine-tuning inter-city movements. Further, the aviation industry's growth in terms of connectivity and the foreign policy of the host government play a key role in promoting tourism, particularly with respect to attracting foreign tourists. As such, a multidimensional approach is required to make Arunachal Pradesh gain visibility on the tourism map as an important destination for domestic and international tourists.

Businesses such as selling agriculture products, dairy products, and farm products, performing cultural events for guests, and selling souvenirs, among others, have a significant economic impact and create a multiplier effect in a host destination. All these small businesses encourage farmers, artisans, and local microenterprises; these are strong support systems for tourism development in destinations. Through tourism's development, local groups can effectively contribute to the welfare of the community.

Social and political empowerment for tourism development is possible only when the economic and psychological well-being of the local community are assured. These elements are interdependent and ensure the smooth development of the destination. Neglecting these measures is like knocking down a stepping stone to growth. As a result, the tourism department should, in a strategic manner, collaborate with interested community members and allied tourism departments through inclusive planning to carry forward tourism development in Arunachal Pradesh.

10.3 Local community as a key stakeholder in tourism development

Many policymakers in the tourism industry consider the local community to be the biggest beneficiary of the benefits that accrue through infrastructural development. Without a doubt, any negative or incorrect actions will have an impact on all local communities and the destination. If the local community is not included as a partner in the process, it could lead to a negative outcome, thereby preventing the achievement of the overall objective of tourism development. The process of tourism development should be considered after careful analysis to be beneficial for hosts and guests.

In recent decades, community participation and its success stories have awed many tourism policymakers and administrators worldwide in terms of economic benefits. As a result, numerous successful projects have emerged, with community participation playing a crucial role in their execution. These projects provided significant benefits to their participating communities through Tourism Revenue Sharing (TRS) programs.

Community participation in tourism occurs in different types of tourism business ventures. However, policymakers and academics frequently associate it with ecotourism, ethnic tourism, village tourism, farm tourism, and agro-tourism. Residents' participation in urban and rural settings also differs in terms of services. In each of these tourism types, the intensity of participation from residents differs from one type to another.

In urban areas, their focus could be on services like casinos, bars, clubs, amusement parks, etc., which have a modern technological touch and are well connected to the lifestyles of the urban population. In rural areas, the focus could be on nature-based activities that are closely associated with rural settings. For example, wildlife areas are near some of the villages in Arunachal Pradesh and naturally encourage rural and cultural tourism.

As mentioned above, the community's social life is the core asset that attracts tourists to the villages. In this regard, the diverse cultural and natural resources of the region may lose their basic identity due to unplanned development. Such negative consequences can be reduced by a common goal and activities preserving the core rural identity.

The tribes of Arunachal Pradesh have not yet experienced mass tourism. Therefore, maintaining the authenticity of social life and culture in their original forms is of utmost importance for the development of the region. Cultural exchange and knowledge of cross-cultural differences must be valued since tourism growth benefits both tourists and local populations. Tourism-friendly governance can help fund cultural programs, preserve history, and encourage community engagement in tourism-related activities in the state.

10.4 Participation of diverse local groups in tourism activities

The development of tourism necessitates the participation of numerous groups and a high level of coordination from all stakeholders, including central, state, and local governments. These include local leaders, SHGs, and other voluntary groups at the village level. From the perspective of tourism entrepreneurship, several resources in rural areas need attention for tourism development in the region.

The tourism industry's nature is multifaceted. Therefore, the engagement of local stakeholders provides ample scope to showcase artefacts, local cuisine, farm practices, community life, and the traditions of rural areas. The rural masses primarily own these opportunities, relying on them for their culture and livelihood. Tourism has the potential to diversify the economy by generating additional income at various levels. For example, tourism revenues can finance conservation efforts and protected area administration while also providing livelihood opportunities to locals. This funding aids in the preservation of natural and cultural treasures for future generations.

Many tourism service businesses approach local communities passively for consultation, with the local community acting primarily as information providers rather than active participants. This results in any project failing to fully maximize its benefits, which in turn affects the initiative's sustainability in tourism destinations. Therefore, any tourism development should include the local community as a key stakeholder in the host destination; it does not necessarily require them to invest in and participate in the tourism business, but as a key host community that accepts tourism development and tourists in their locality.

10.5 Recommendation for potential tourism development

The existing tourism infrastructure and facilities lacked modern amenities and could not cater to large tourist inflows. However, the state's socio-cultural diversity can potentially cater to responsible tourism activities. Both the natural and cultural resources of the state have the attractions to create Special Interest Tourism (SIT) activities. For example, the state tourism department can collaborate with other educational institutes for educational tours and research projects to boost tourism and preserve culture and traditions.

The concerned department must also carefully choose its Tourism Brand Ambassador for the state. The officials must critically analyse how the ambassador may represent the state without any political or vested interests. The chosen person must foster a positive image for the state, inspire the local youths, and promote the state in the best possible ways. Arunachal Pradesh has a serene landscape, picturesque hills and valleys, and a pleasant climate. All these complement its hospitable people, rich heritage of arts and crafts, and colourful festivals that reflect its close connection with rich culture and nature. The vibrant tribal life of 26 major and 100 plus subtribes makes the state an emerging destination for cultural tourism.

Visitors often refer to the state as 'Mini India' due to its ethnic and distinct socio-cultural context. Therefore, appropriate translation of the state's resources into tourism goods and services is crucial. To some extent, proper integration of local tourism firms will help to improve socioeconomic status. The state also has the lowest population density in the country (India), with 17 persons per square km (Census, 2011). If professionally managed, the low population in the state may create a conducive environment with good carrying capacity and a promising ecosystem for tourism development.

Rural tourism, cultural tourism, ecotourism, and a few adventure tourism activities are already happening in the state; however, there is potential for other forms of tourism. The list of other potential tourism types is for the study area. This recommendation and tourism types can also be adopted by any other similar destination in the world. The list include:

10.5.1 Agri-tourism/farm tourism

Agri-tourism refers to a type of tourism that involves visiting and experiencing farms, ranches, or other agricultural settings for recreational purposes. This can include activities such as picking fruits and vegetables, taking farm tours, and even participating in agricultural activities like harvesting.

Agri-tourism aims to promote rural development, support local farmers, and foster a deeper understanding and appreciation of agriculture and the natural environment. It also provides an opportunity for tourists to engage with nature and experience the country's rural culture firsthand. The vast majority of rural populations in the state are still active in farming, and agri-tourism can be promoted in this regard.

10.5.2 Religious Tourism and Pilgrimage tourism

Religious tourism refers to travel motivated by a person's interest in visiting sites or experiencing cultures that are significant to their specific faith or beliefs. This type of tourism allows individuals to connect with their spiritual roots, immerse themselves in revered rituals, and explore the historical significance of sacred sites. Tourist sites like Tawang Monastery, Parshuram Kund, etc., can be highlighted for both domestic and international tourists in this category.

Pilgrimage tourism is a specific type of travel where individuals visit a sacred site or location as a spiritual journey. This type of tourism is often characterized by a physical or emotional journey, where the traveler is seeking a deeper connection with their faith or a higher power.

10.5.3 Doom Tourism

The term 'doom tourism' or 'last-chance' is the phenomenon of the desire for tourists to witness vanishing landscapes or seascapes, a last chance to witness a special feature or event, disappearing species, etc. When a certain site becomes sufficiently endangered, it may also increase the demand to go and see it. For example, the last living generation of Apatani Facial Tattoo can be promoted in this regard.

10.5.4 Rural Tourism

Rural tourism refers to the act of visiting and exploring rural areas, such as countryside, villages, and small towns, to experience the local culture, traditions, and way of life. It is a growing trend in tourism that focuses on immersing visitors in the natural environment and interacting with local communities.

10.5.5 Educational Tourism

Educational tourism, also known as educational travel, refers to a type of tourism that involves traveling to learn about a particular place, culture, history, or subject matter. In this form of tourism, the educational aspect is the primary purpose of travel. It is a way to combine leisure and education, allowing individuals to explore new places and gain knowledge while on vacation. Educational tourism can take many forms, such as cultural immersion programs, study abroad trips, and language exchange opportunities. As mentioned before, the state holds many unique cultural and natural resources that can be promoted for educational-specific purposes.

10.5.6 Ethnic Tourism

Ethnic tourism refers to a type of travel that focuses on experiencing and learning about the culture, traditions, and ways of life of local ethnic groups. It involves visiting indigenous communities, participating in their customs, and immersing oneself in their daily routines. Ethnic tourism aims to promote cross-cultural understanding, preserve traditional practices, and provide economic benefits to local communities. The state is home to many diverse tribes with distinct practices in terms of belief, dress, cuisine, culture, etc. It is observed that the concerned department has integrated this element into promotional activities to some extent.

10.5.7 Wine Tourism

Wine tourism refers to the practice of traveling to wine-producing regions to experience the culture, history, and production of wine. This can include wine tastings, vineyard tours, and educational workshops. Wine tourism has become a significant sector of the tourism industry, with many destinations offering wine-themed experiences, such as wine-paired meals, wine-making classes. This includes, visiting vineyards, wineries, tasting, consuming and/or purchasing wine, etc. The recent development of wine manufacturing units in the state should be collaborated on this regard.

10.5.8 Avi-tourism

Avi-tourism refers to a type of ecotourism that focuses on birdwatching and the conservation of bird species. It involves traveling to specific locations to observe and learn about birds in their natural habitats. This often supports local economies and promotes sustainable tourism practices. Bird enthusiasts, ornithologists, and conservationists participate in avitourism to study, photograph, and appreciate the diversity of bird species.

Avi-tourism is currently only taking place in very few regions of the state, but it has the potential to expand to other parts of the state. This type of tourism needs trained local guides who understand the local region and are also sensitive to local culture and its close connection with nature, so the process does not harm the sentiments of local people. It can involve guided birdwatching tours, scientific study, providing opportunities for regular visitors to watch, and other educational forms of tourism. It is a highly specialized sector of nature-based tourism and is usually fixed on viewing avian species in their natural settings.

10.5.9 Military Tourism

Military tourism, also known as military adventure tourism, involves visiting and experiencing military-related destinations, events, or activities, such as battlefield tours, military museums, and war memorials. It allows civilians to gain insight into military culture, history, and operations.

This may also include visiting current or historic military sites and facilities, including museums, battlefields, cemeteries, technology related to the military, etc.

10.5.10 Border Tourism

Border tourism refers to the growing trend of tourists visiting and exploring border regions between countries. This type of tourism often focuses on experiencing the cultural, historical, and natural attractions unique to these areas. Border regions can offer a distinctive blend of border towns, customs, and traditions, making them an attractive destinations for adventurous travellers. Examples of popular border tourism destinations include India-Pakistan, India-Tibet, China, the US-Mexico border, the England-Wales border, the France-Spain border, etc.

The rich biodiversity and culture of the state should be explored more through tourism; the potential for tourism development is not limited to the above-mentioned. However, the concerned regions' development authorities can introduce them based on the available tourism resources.

Visits for study-related purposes in the state may be encouraged through educational tourism and excursions. Action-driven activities like trying local handloom and craft items may be promoted through homestays and crafts centres for a better experience for the tourists. These activities create value for the natural and human-made resources in the destination.

10.6 An inclusive model for community participation in tourism development

Community participation and the promotion of rural tourism are highly dependent on the destination's socio-cultural and environmental factors. In many rural tourist destinations, there is a significant gap in the participation of the local community in tourism and allied services. The local community is often unaware of tourism business opportunities due to a lack of education and general awareness. Those who volunteer to participate in certain initiatives, such as homestay services, learn about the opportunities only after attending tourism-related programs and forums. This led to a greater requirement to organize awareness camps for the local community.

Further, community participation and rural tourism are often associated with pro-poor tourism. Connecting the local community with the global economy through the tourism industry is a widely accepted interpretation. Now, coming back to the study area, despite the state's rich diversity and being one of the most vital biodiversity hotspots globally, the state's potential in terms of tourism has not yet been explored much. Further, 34.67 per cent of people in Arunachal Pradesh are below the poverty line, which is much higher than the national average of 21.92 per cent as per the 2011 census report of India.

The current economic conditions in Arunachal Pradesh necessitate significant intervention, particularly by locals in the tourism industry. This sector presents a viable alternative for job generation and has the potential to mitigate poverty to some extent. As previously mentioned, the study also outlines the obstacles to tourism and the essential support systems needed to surmount them, thereby promoting greater participation from the local community. Therefore, based on the findings, the study recommends a model for inclusive community participation in tourism **(Table 10.1) and (Table 10.2)** indicates support systems require from the government. However, we can implement and adopt the model in other destinations that face similar challenges in tourism development. We can incorporate and modify a few more elements according to the tourism development and strategies required in those locations.

Table 10.1 Model for community participation in tourism development

Stage-I Understand the existing level of tourism development and its barriers	Stage-II Creating conducive environments for tourism service providers	Stage-III Executive plans and development	Stage-IV Create help desk service	
• Nature of participation in tourism • Types of tourism products and services • Level of infrastructural development in tourism • Operational structure of business • Socio-cultural aspects of tourism development (both positive and negative sides) • Field observations • Check necessary data in tourism development, etc.	• Nature and types of tourism development • Barriers to tourism development • Integration of locals • Marketing patterns of tourism products and service • Types of tourism products and services • Professional experience of locals • Field study and observations • Opinion of non-participants in tourism, etc.	Identify and focus on a specific or multiple areas to work on in each segment .	• Focus on identified issues • Create programs/capacity building that solve the issues identified • Development plan on priority basis and destination-specific requirement • Create schemes/assistance for immediate support wherever possible. • Stage four is the crucial stage that competent officials and personnel should handle.	**Stage -V** Conducts awareness camps/forums **Stage -VI** Field observations, collect feedback for possible improvement **Stage -VII** Outcomes • Professional satisfaction of locals in tourism business • Willingness to continue in the profession • Benefits of tourism development in different segments and allied industry.

10.6.1 Stage I: Understand the existing level of tourism development and its barriers

The first stage as shown in **Table 10.1**, should involve an understanding of the existing nature, demand, phases, and problems of tourism development in various dimensions. These may include the nature and type of local community participation in tourism development. Barriers to community participation in tourism include the integration of local tourism service providers in the development of tourism marketing opportunities for community-produced and owned tourism products and services. This also includes local service providers' views and concerns about their tourism development and experiences.

Table 10.2 Support systems require from the government for tourism development

	Support systems for tourism development
Govt. backed initiatives	<ul><li>Tourism policy</li><li>Pro-tourism governance</li><li>A tourism-friendly administration or system</li><li>Tourism friendly officials (pro-tourism officials)</li><li>Tourism-friendly local community</li></ul>

To create a favourable business climate, the state's administration and various allied departments should collaborate on the development of tourism infrastructure. For example, addressing key barriers to tourism development for local tourism firms and other necessary facilities like telecommunication facilities, connectivity, and sanitation facilities at all the designated tourist sites and important transit points should be improved and built wherever necessary.

10.6.2 Stage II: Creating a conducive environment for service providers

10.6.2.1: Training and capacity buildings programs

Service providers, regardless of the nature and types of activities they engage in, require effective communication about training and capacity-building programs related to tourism. There are many opportunities in catering businesses, as well as in tourist guides and accommodation services. Therefore, the tourism department must create focused development plans and conduct training programs for skill enhancement based on the needs of the service providers. Furthermore, service providers require basic training primarily in marketing and branding. Aside from that, there is also a need for assistance from the tourism department and the relevant government.

10.6.2.2: Tourism Policy

The study shows that having a friendly socio-cultural environment is not enough to make a good tourism destination. For a tourism firm to operate smoothly, it is required to **identify and select appropriate tasks to initiate.** Facilities and amenities must be provided. The tourism department should draft a viable tourism policy for Arunachal Pradesh, taking into account the socio-cultural aspects of locals and an in-depth understanding of the nature of tourism resources, in order to create a better ecosystem for the tourism industry to flourish.

It is time that the central and state governments investigate all issues related to tourism development highlighted in this report and work hand in hand for the greater good. By collaborating with local service providers, the Directorate of Tourism, Govt. of Arunachal Pradesh, can focus on micro-level planning for tourism development in the region, enhancing the platform for tourists to access tourism-related information and implementing innovative solutions to address any shortcomings in host-guest issues. The region requires a dedicated micro- and macro-level approach to infrastructure planning to overcome hurdles related to transportation.

10.6.2.3: Pro-tourism governance

A peaceful political climate and support system from the local government are of utmost importance. Unrest and political instability are less conducive to making headway in tourism as investors do not come forward to invest in tourism ventures. The role of power and the relationship between different government bodies' interests have a significant impact on the overall development of the business environment. Pro-tourism government initiatives such as visa on arrival and speeding up the visa process make the destinations tourist-friendly with fewer procedural hustles.

Pro-tourism governance fosters sustainable tourism development and maximizes the positive impacts of tourism on destinations. Tourism is a significant contributor to employment opportunities, economic development, revenue generation, and foreign currency in the host country. Governance that is favourable to tourism ensures that tourism policies and strategies are intended to maximize economic benefits and encourage investment in the sector. Tourism development can serve as a conduit for fostering peace and understanding among diverse nations and cultures. Pro-tourism governance also promotes peace and understanding. It contributes to the development of the tourism industry and can facilitate international cooperation and communication, resulting in better diplomatic relations.

10.6.2.4: Pro-tourism administration

Pro-tourism administration here refers to a government's efforts to promote and develop the tourism industry in an area or country. This involves implementing policies and strategies to attract visitors, create tourist-friendly infrastructure, and ensure a positive experience for tourists. Effective pro-tourism administration can boost local economies, create jobs, and preserve cultural heritage sites.

In many cases, a pro-tourism administration is a collaborative effort between government agencies, private-sector businesses, and local communities. A tourism-friendly administration promotes the preservation and promotion of cultural heritage sites and practices. This can assist in preserving local identity, fostering local pride, and attracting tourists interested in authentic cultural experiences.

10.6.2.5: Pro-tourism officials

The pro-tourism officials ensure the development and management of tourism in a sustainable, accountable, and equitable manner in their day-to-day official work and developmental activities related to tourism.

It seeks to maximize the positive impacts of tourism while minimizing its negative effects, thereby creating an environment in which vacationers, host communities, and the environment all benefit from tourism development.

10.6.3 Stage III: Executive Plans and Development of Tourism Infrastructure

The state is in immediate need of better basic infrastructure to scale new heights in the tourism industry. Therefore, state and central governments, on a priority basis, focus on improving infrastructure facilities, especially with respect to road networks, air connectivity, and rail connectivity, among others. Executive plans and development can also be focused on identified tourist circuits (as given in Chapter one) for further improvements in tourism infrastructure.

Instead of a one-shot activity, on a continuous basis, necessary follow-up measures need to be in place in overall planning and development. It is observed that government machinery somehow motivates and assists in the initial stage but fails to follow up in the later stages. This led to an absence of mechanisms where service providers are not connected to the market in a systematic way.

10.6.4 Stage IV: Initiate the Help Desk Service

There is a need to strengthen the distribution mechanism for community-produced and owned tourism products and services. It's observed that tourism authorities somehow motivate and assist locals, but to make their initiative effective, follow-up should happen on an interval basis.

As a result, service providers end up without customers due to a lack of knowledge and skills to promote their products and services in the market. Therefore, creating a help desk for converting local communities' resources into tourism products and services is the need of the hour. Indigenous knowledge bases may be used and transformed into tourism resources, which can lead to a better way of creating livelihoods without fear of losing cultural identity.

10.6.5 Stage V: Awareness camps and public forums on developmental schemes and benefits

The government must create awareness about tourism schemes and projects at the village level with detailed explanations and interpretations in the local dialect for a clear understanding of the local community. Only then can schemes related to tourism in the region reach the maximum number of people at the grass-roots level for better and more active participation.

The right information regarding training and capacity-building programs related to tourism needs to be well communicated to the participants. Therefore, the tourism department must pay immediate attention to it. Disbursement of financial assistance and awareness of schemes related to tourism need to reach out to the beneficiaries without bias and on a need-based basis. The role of information and awareness about tourism opportunities is crucial to public participation. True engagement in business requires complete information about the market of the industry. These problems are frequently observed in many other regions of developing countries.

Overall, quite often local communities lack basic business skills and, as a result, find it difficult to sustain their businesses, particularly in rural, remote destinations where modern amenities are not well established. The business units from such places mostly keep a low profile, and the businesses also run in a low-key manner.

The current study found many challenging issues for the local community that need immediate interventions from concerned authorities for inclusive tourism development. Therefore, a thorough analysis of the findings suggests that the Directorate of Tourism, Govt. of Arunachal Pradesh, actively address these issues to ensure smooth business operations.

10.6.6 Stage VI: Field observation, seek feedback for improvements, and how the initiative benefits

In this stage, critical observation is required on the real benefits of initiatives executed in the tourism destination. This includes feedback from the ground report and beneficiaries. This information is required to assist or reduce potential barriers, financial aid, schemes, capacity building, and assistance in the development of tourism products and services.

These factors are significant in promoting tourism development and building a willingness amongst service providers to continue in the profession. The professional satisfaction of locals in tourism businesses and the benefits of tourism development will reflect in different segments of tourism and allied industries, as mentioned on **stage VII.** The whole process of tourism development requires a government-backed support system (**Table 10.2**), and all stages as described in **Table 10.1.**

The feedback can be used to improve execution or alter any development plans. And the review process can be started over at *stage I* if needed to revisit the issues raised, barriers in the process, and the whole process of development.

10.7 Summary

Most of the time, rural communities participate in tourism development passively, relying solely on consultation and resource gathering. In this regard, it is desirable that local tourism entrepreneurs be involved in such forums and meetings to enable them to express their views and perspectives on tourism development.

The local community is a treasure trove of culture for tourists who seek authentic service and experience from the host community. These services can be in any form; for example, homestay services can offer a different experience to tourists in their traditional manner. Simultaneously, accommodations such as model villages, huts, and community lodging areas may overlook certain aspects when compared to the experience offered by homestay services.

Since the **study's findings bring out barriers in the tourism industry**, a thorough understanding of the barriers can help practitioners and policymakers investigate the matter with action focused. The findings may help in implementing tourism projects in destinations with similar contexts by considering the local community's resources for tourism and related businesses.

The result output of the current study is also applicable to other destinations because the methods are rigorous, and include empirical confirmation of the infrastructural support system, a thorough understanding of the service providers both on quantitative and qualitative aspects of parameters such as operational barriers, understanding possible socio-cultural barriers, and assessing personal barriers, if any, to participation at any level from different professions in the tourism and related sectors.

The study contributes to understanding local tourism service providers and their perspectives on various dimensions of tourism development. Accordingly, policymakers and industry practitioners may create a business-friendly environment and curate a region-specific model for tourism development. **The tourism industry is one of the prominent drivers of rapid economic growth**.

Many countries, both developed and developing, have acknowledged the community as a stakeholder in tourism development and initiated various projects and schemes involving community participation in tourism. Such initiatives and schemes primarily focus on integrating the community into the tourism industry. Therefore, policymakers should initiate the necessary programs, training, and schemes for better inclusion. Ensure smooth business operations and good revenue at the destination. Giving local tourism firms more control over the development and delivery of services automatically decreases the involvement of outside parties.

Awareness raised through motivation adds value to the process and establishes a chain of activities, which is critical for **capacity-building initiatives**, especially in rural areas where community-based tourism projects and schemes are cantered on the rural sector. Therefore, community tourism firms should be provided with a dedicated and exclusive help desk for assistance in business operations, which may act as a one-stop service facilitation centre for information about schemes and projects concerning tourism and allied services.

The tourism development requires attention from tourism regulatory bodies in light of its rich resources for tourism. Through this study and with proper guidance and channelization of resources, the tourism industry of the region can be uplifted to support the local economy and preserve local culture. The analysis and findings of the study **brought out the barriers that** affect community tourism services in different categories.

Identification and a thorough understanding of the barriers can enable policymakers to come up with solutions to problems that could be effectively addressed. These specific challenges and suggestions may uniquely arise for each destination. The government should **channel local tourism products and services into more viable** operations that are easily accessible to customers. Establishing an exclusive help desk for the local community is an important step in the right direction, as the region is still in the early stages of tourism growth with limited marketing infrastructure.

The accessibility issues and their effect on the region's tourism development need constant support and cooperation. Another subject worth mentioning is the understanding of **socio-cultural aspects of marketing and their effect on brand** value creation in the community and rural tourism resources.

Policymakers must undserstand the barriers to tourism development, which include socio-cultural, infrastructural, operational, and personal barriers, to effectively execute tourism projects. This study is the first study on community participation in tourism as a case study in Arunachal Pradesh. This study brings out scopes to understand existing challenges. The book is also intended to help scholars, service providers, and governing bodies related to tourism from other regions or countries that focus on rural tourism, community participation, and developing any new tourism destination.

In addition to the points mentioned in this chapter, the state must not only gain visibility on the tourism map of the country but also in the international tourism market. Arunachal Pradesh requires a collaborative approach from various stakeholders in the region, including NGOs, SHGs, interest groups, the government's machinery, the local community, and other departments that are closely related to tourism development. The tourism resources of the region, such as artefacts, local cuisine, farm practices, and community life, may be put to optimal use by converting the resources into sources of livelihood through tourism.

Recognizing the **challenges faced by first-generation tourism service** providers would assist in project formulation at emerging tourist destinations. Future research can also lead to a deeper understanding of the various types of tourism barriers in different regions and communities. This research brings into focus and assists in the better implementation of tourism-related schemes and initiatives for the local community.

The analysis of new opportunities in various forms of tourism may lead to the creation of the necessary workforce for the region's tourism development, as we have discussed in other chapters of the book. Depending on the circumstances, interests, and availability of the destination's resources, the study could also assist governmental bodies in building a support system for tourism projects.

10.8 Conclusion and future directions

Policymakers, practitioners, and scholars can use the recommendations and guidelines provided in this book to plan tourism development, understand the challenges of rural tourism and the community, and conduct scholarly research in the domain. However, there can be minor or major modifications as per specific needs in other destinations.

All research stages, challenges, and findings in this book should act like easy reference points. These include stepwise research process, several suggestions, major findings, implementations, and action points designed to tackle significant barriers and potential tools to promote tourism industry while keeping the local community in mind.

The significance of establishing a tourism strategy and the model for tourism development needs to be checked and revised wherever neccessary in future studies, as society and market, as well as levels of demand and development in the tourism industry, are constantly changing. The model for tourism development and its stages can serve as reference points for similar tourism destinations and are highly useful for policymakers and practitioners in tourism and allied industries.

The stages of the research process and different parameters given in the book are useful for any scholars who are interested in conducting in-depth research in tourism development and local communities to understand various dimensions of challenges.

The recommendations and directions in this book are to stimulate collaboration and share knowledge with fellow researchers, practitioners, entrepreneurs, and policymakers. In addition, the motive behind writing this book and using the data from the case study is to encourage open communication, foster a better business ecosystem for the tourism industry, and encourage community participation in the industry.

****

Bibliography

Acharya, B. P., & Halpenny, E. A. (2013). Homestays as an alternative tourism product for sustainable community development: A case study of women-managed tourism product in rural Nepal. *Tourism Planning & Development, 10*(4), 367-387.

Amir, A. F., Ghapar, A. A., Jamal, S. A., & Ahmad, K. N. (2015). Sustainable Tourism Development: A Study on Community Resilience for Rural Tourism in Malaysia. *Procedia - Social and Behavioral Sciences, 168*, 116–122. https://doi.org/10.1016/j.sbspro.2014.10.217

Briedenhann, J. and Wickens, E., 2004. Tourism routes as a tool for the economic development of rural areas—vibrant hope or impossible dream?. *Tourism management, 25*(1), pp.71-79.

Brouder, P., & Eriksson, R. H. (2013). Staying Power: What Influences Micro-firm Survival in Tourism? Tourism Geographies, 15(1), 125–144. https://doi.org/10.1080/14616688.2011.647326

Census of India (2011). *Provisional Population Totals. New Delhi: Government of India*, 409-413. http://censusindia.gov.in/2011-proresults/paper2/prov_results_paper2_india.html

Census of India. (2011). Provisional Population Totals Paper 1 of Arunachal Pradesh - 2011. Retrieved from https://censusindia.gov.in/2011-prov-results/prov_data_products_arunachal.html

Chang, H. L., Chou, Y. C., Wu, D. Y., & Wu, S. C. (2018). Will firm's marketing efforts on owned social media payoff? A quasi-experimental analysis of tourism products. *Decision Support Systems, 107*, 13–25. https://doi.org/10.1016/j.dss.2017.12.011

Chiutsi, S., & Saarinen, J. (2017). Local participation in transfrontier tourism: Case of Sengwe community in Great Limpopo Transfrontier Conservation Area, Zimbabwe. *Development Southern Africa, 34*(3), 260–275. https://doi.org/10.1080/0376835X.2016.1259987

Choi, H. C., & Murray, I. (2010). Resident attitudes toward sustainable community tourism. Journal of Sustainable Tourism, 18(4), 575–594. https://doi.org/10.1080/09669580903524852

Cole, S. (2006). Information and empowerment: The keys to achieving sustainable tourism. *Journal of sustainable tourism, 14*(6), 629-644.

Coros, M. M., Gica, O. A., Yallop, A. C., & Moisescu, O. I. (2017). Innovative and sustainable tourism strategies: a viable alternative for Romania's economic development. Worldwide Hospitality and Tourism Themes. https://doi.org/10.1108/WHATT-07-2017-0033

Dey, B., & Sarma, M. K. (2010). Information source usage among motive-based segments of travelers to newly emerging tourist destinations. *Tourism Management, 31*(3), 341–344. https://doi.org/10.1016/j.tourman.2009.03.015

Echtner, C. M., & Prasad, P. (2003). The context of third world tourism marketing. *Annals of Tourism Research, 30*(3), 660–682. https://doi.org/10.1016/S0160-7383(03)00045-8

Eshliki, S. A., & Kaboudi, M. (2012). Community Perception of Tourism Impacts and Their Participation in Tourism Planning: A Case Study of Ramsar, Iran. *Procedia - Social and Behavioral Sciences.* https://doi.org/10.1016/j.sbspro.2012.03.037

Forest Survey of India (2019) https://fsi.nic.in/isfr-volume-i?pgID=isfr-volume-i

Forstner, K. (2004). Community ventures and access to markets: The role of intermediaries in marketing rural tourism products. Development Policy Review, 22(5), 497–514. https://doi.org/10.1111/j.1467-7679.2004.00262.x

Goodwin, H. (2002). Local community involvement in tourism around National Parks: Opportunities and constraints. Current Issues in Tourism, 5(3–4), 338–360. https://doi.org/10.1080/13683500208667928

Gurung, D. B., & Seeland, K. (2008). Ecotourism in Bhutan. Extending its Benefits to Rural Communities. Annals of Tourism Research. https://doi.org/10.1016/j.annals.2008.02.004

Kachniewska, M. A. (2015). Tourism development as a determinant of quality of life in rural areas. Worldwide Hospitality and Tourism Themes. https://doi.org/10.1108/WHATT-06-2015-0028

Kala, D., & Bagri, S. C. (2018). Barriers to local community participation in tourism development: Evidence from mountainous state Uttarakhand, India. *Tourism: An International Interdisciplinary Journal, 66*(3), 318-333.

Luo, S. W., & Lee, Y. C. (2017). A research on community participation in eco-tourism of aboriginal people in Taiwan. Proceedings of the IEEE International Conference on Advanced Materials for Science and Engineering: Innovation, Science and Engineering, IEEE-ICAMSE 2016, (1), 23–26. https://doi.org/10.1109/ICAMSE.2016.7840221

Mak, B.K., Cheung, L.T. and Hui, D.L., 2017. Community participation in the decision-making process for sustainable tourism development in rural areas of Hong Kong, China. Sustainability, 9(10), p.1695. https://doi.org/10.3390/su9101695

Malek, A., & Costa, C. (2015). Integrating Communities into Tourism Planning Through Social Innovation. *Tourism Planning and Development, 12*(3), 281–299. https://doi.org/10.1080/21568316.2014.951125

Mangold, W. G., & Faulds, D. J. (2009). Social media: The new hybrid element of the promotion mix. *Business Horizons, 52*(4), 357–365. https://doi.org/10.1016/j.bushor.2009.03.002

Mize, T., Kanwal, K. S., Rangini, N., Yama, L., Patuk, O., & Lodhi, M. S. (2016). The current development of ecotourism in Ziro Valley and its significance in Arunachal Pradesh, India. *Int J Adv Res Innov Ideas Educ, 2*(6), 1735-1743.

Moertini, V. S. (2012). Small Medium Enterprises: On Utilizing Business-to-Business e-Commerce to Go Global. *Procedia Economics and Finance*, *4*(Icsmed), 13–22. https://doi.org/10.1016/s2212-5671(12)00316-4

Moscardo, G., Konovalov, E., Murphy, L., & McGehee, N. (2013). Mobilities, community well-being and sustainable tourism. Journal of Sustainable Tourism, 21(4), 532–556. https://doi.org/10.1080/09669582.2013.785556

Munar, A. M. (2012). Social Media Strategies and Destination Management. Scandinavian Journal of Hospitality and Tourism, 12(2), 101–120. https://doi.org/10.1080/15022250.2012.679047

Neto, F. (2003). A new approach to sustainable tourism development: Moving beyond environmental protection. Natural Resources Forum, 27(3), 212–222. https://doi.org/10.1111/1477-8947.00056

Patowary, B., & Borgohain, P. (2017). Community participation in sustainable tourism development in ziro valley of Arunachal Pradesh. *International Journal of Research in Social Sciences*, 7(6), 193-203.

Prince, S. (2017). Craft-art in the Danish countryside: reconciling a lifestyle, livelihood and artistic career through rural tourism. Journal of Tourism and Cultural Change, 15(4), 339–358. https://doi.org/10.1080/14766825.2016.1154064

Saarinen, J., & Lenao, M. (2014). Integrating tourism to rural development and planning in the developing world. *Development Southern Africa, 31*(3), 363–372. https://doi.org/10.1080/0376835X.2014.888334

Saufi, A., O'Brien, D., & Wilkins, H. (2014). Inhibitors to host community participation in sustainable tourism development in developing countries. Journal of Sustainable Tourism, 22(5), 801–820. https://doi.org/10.1080/09669582.2013.861468

Saxena, G., & Ilbery, B. (2008). Integrated rural tourism a border case study. *Annals of Tourism Research, 35*(1), 233–254. https://doi.org/10.1016/j.annals.2007.07.010

Seeland, K. (2008). ECOTOURISM IN BHUTAN Extending its Benefits to Rural Communities, 35(2), 489–508. https://doi.org/10.1016/j.annals.2008.02.004

Shen, F., Hughey, K. F. D., & Simmons, D. G. (2008). Connecting the sustainable livelihoods approach and tourism: A review of the literature. *Journal of Hospitality and Tourism Management, 15*(1), 19–31. https://doi.org/10.1375/jhtm.15.19

Sood, J., Lynch, P., & Anastasiadou, C. (2017). Community non-participation in homestays in Kullu, Himachal Pradesh, India. Tourism Management, 60, 332–347. https://doi.org/10.1016/j.tourman.2016.12.007

Stem, C. J., Lassoie, J. P., Lee, D. R., & Deshler, D. J. (2003). How'eco'is ecotourism? A comparative case study of ecotourism in Costa Rica. *Journal of sustainable tourism, 11*(4), 322-347.

Su, M. M., Wall, G., Wang, Y., & Jin, M. (2019). Livelihood sustainability in a rural tourism destination - Hetu Town, Anhui Province, China. Tourism Management, 71(October 2018), 272–281.

https://doi.org/10.1016/j.tourman.2018.10.019

Survey of India (2023). State Maps. Arunachal Pradesh. https://surveyofindia.gov.in/documents/uploads/document-50780-arunachal-state-map.jpg. Accessed on 29th May 2023

Sutawa, G. K. (2012). Issues on Bali Tourism Development and Community Empowerment to Support Sustainable Tourism Development. *Procedia Economics and Finance*, 4(Icsmed), 413–422. https://doi.org/10.1016/s2212-5671(12)00356-5

Timothy, D. J. (1999). Participatory planningA view of tourism in Indonesia. *Annals of tourism research*, 26(2), 371-391.

Tosun, C. (2000). Limits to community participation in the tourism development process in developing countries. *Tourism management*, 21(6), 613-633.

Tosun, C., & Jenkins, C. L. (1998). Planning in third-world countries: a critique. *Progress in Tourism and Hospitality Research*, 4, 101–114.

Triantafillidou, E. and Tsiaras, S. (2018) 'Exploring entrepreneurship, innovation and tourism development from a sustainable perspective: Evidence from Greece', *Journal for International Business and Entrepreneurship Development*, Vol. 11, No. 1, pp.53–64.

Wang, Y., Yu, Q., & Fesenmaier, D. R. (2002). Defining the virtual tourist community: Implications for tourism marketing. *Tourism Management*, 23(4), 407–417.

Yaja, M., & Kumar, A. (2021). An empirical study of marketing of SMEs in the tourism sector. *Small Enterprise Research*, 0(0), 1–15. https://doi.org/10.1080/13215906.2021.1962396

Yaja, M. (2021) Community participation in tourism a case study of Arunachal Pradesh (Doctoral dissertation). Pondicherry University. Retrieve from https://shodhganga.inflibnet.ac.in/

Zeng, B., & Gerritsen, R. (2014). What do we know about social media in tourism? A review. *Tourism Management Perspectives*, 10, 27–36. https://doi.org/10.1016/j.tmp.2014.01.001

Ziipao, R. R. (2018). Look/Act east policy, roads and market infrastructure in North-East India. *Strategic Analysis*, 42(5), 476-489.